D1024865

Emily Brontë

Twayne's English Authors Series

Herbert Sussman, Editor
Northeastern University

TEAS 326

The Brontë home at Haworth (with the addition of
the Brontë Parsonage Museum) today.
From a photograph by the author

Emily Brontë

By Richard Benvenuto

Michigan State University

Twayne Publishers • *Boston*

Emily Brontë

Richard Benvenuto

Copyright © 1982 by G. K. Hall & Co.
Published by Twayne Publishers
A Division of G. K. Hall & Company
70 Lincoln Street
Boston, Massachusetts 02111

Book Production by Marne B. Sultz

Book Design by Barbara Anderson

Printed on permanent/durable acid-free
paper and bound in the United States of
America.

**Library of Congress Cataloging in
Publication Data**

Benvenuto, Richard.
Emily Brontë.

(Twayne's English authors series : TEAS
326)
Bibliography: pp. 136–143
Includes index.
1. Bronte, Emily, 1818–1848
—Criticism and interpretation.
I. Title. II. Series.
PR4173.B46   823'.8   81-20032
ISBN 0-8057-6813-0   AACR2

Contents

About the Author

Richard Benvenuto received the B.A. from the University of Detroit, the M.A. from Hollins College, Virginia, and the Ph.D. from Ohio State University. A member of the English Department at Michigan State University since 1968, he is now an associate professor of English, and has published articles on Charlotte Brontë, Robert Browning, Ernest Dowson, Gissing, Keats, and Hardy. In 1973–74, he participated in a teacher-exchange program and taught at the University of Leeds, close to the heart of the Brontë country.

Preface

Emily Brontë was an obscure, virtually unknown author when she died in 1848, and even now, despite the numerous biographies of her that have been written, there are still large portions of her life that we know little about. For her personality, even her appearance, we must rely largely on conjecture. Her one novel and most famous work, *Wuthering Heights,* has always been controversial, and critical interpretations of it continue to differ widely. Perhaps the one point on which the vast majority of its readers do agree is that it is not a superficial book—just as no one today questions Brontë's right to be ranked among the great Victorian writers.

There is some question as to how much of Brontë's life is revealed in her art, but for the most part I treat her life and her literary work separately. Brontë developed an objective, dramatic art which enabled her to create imaginary characters and to take on and express their different points of view—and thus shield her private self. But interest in her life remains high, and in my biographical chapter I record what is known and what can be reasonably inferred about Brontë the person. With practically all of her letters and other personal documents destroyed or lost, Brontë has been generally treated as a sphinx or an enigma. While I have felt and do acknowledge the mystery that is Emily Brontë, my aim was to present her as perhaps the most fiercely independent member of a remarkable family—a woman of considerable strength, who could be both a practical housekeeper and a mystic.

Brontë wrote a great deal more than *Wuthering Heights.* For most of her adult life she collaborated with Anne Brontë, her sister, in the creation of an epic saga about an imaginary people they called the Gondalans. My chapter on Gondal reconstructs what is known about this private myth, and following the example of the best commentators on the Gondal material, I have tried to distinguish between the provable and the conjectural. The Gondal story, extending throughout Brontë's formative years, had a major influence on the development of her imagination. Much of the poetry Brontë wrote in the ten years before *Wuthering Heights* pertains to Gondal. Her poetry shows very real, if not always consistent, skill and power, and it has been generally underrated. My third chapter assesses Brontë's achievement as a poet, and concentrates on her technical experiments and devices as well as on the thematic content and pattern of ideas in her poetry as a whole. I include a discussion of Brontë's French essays in order to cover all of her known work, and because in the essays Brontë comes as close as she ever does to speaking in her own voice and to revealing the person behind the artist.

Wuthering Heights has been read and interpreted in numerous ways. It has become a central text for the historian of ideas, the moral and the myth critic, the Marxist and the Freudian critic. In my reading of Brontë's masterpiece, rather than advancing one thesis only, I have tried to suggest various approaches to it; and I have drawn upon some of the best criticism, both when it agrees with and differs from my own perceptions and conclusions. My intention was to give a comprehensive view of *Wuthering Heights,* one that would serve to guide the general reader to what is most important in Brontë's novel and interest the specialist as well.

Most of the critical writings on Emily Brontë have appeared as articles or as separate chapters in books dealing with the Brontës as a whole or with such topics as English fiction or Victorian literature. There have been relatively few books written on her alone and fewer still that address themselves both to her life and all of her work. It is the purpose and intention of this volume to present Brontë and all of her work fully and fairly.

Richard Benvenuto

Michigan State University

Acknowledgments

Quotations from Winifred Gérin, *Emily Brontë: A Biography* (1971), and from the Clarendon Edition of *Wuthering Heights,* edited by Hilda Marsden, Inga-Stina Ewbank, and Ian Jack (1976), are by permission of Oxford University Press. Acknowledgment is also made to Columbia University Press for permission to quote from *The Complete Poems of Emily Jane Brontë.*

Chronology

1843   Alone at Haworth with her father; a time of creativity and freedom.

1844   Begins to arrange her poems into two notebooks, dividing the Gondalan from the non-Gondalan material.

1845   The Brontës give up hopes for a school of their own; Branwell, working on a novel, tells his sisters of the profitable possibilities of novel writing; Emily's birthday note shows her hearty and content, reunited with Anne and as enthusiastic as ever about the Gondalans; October, Charlotte discovers Emily's poems and convinces her sister to collaborate on a volume of poems; December, *Wuthering Heights* begun.

1846   May, *Poems by Currer, Ellis, and Acton Bell* published, with the Brontës paying for costs; July, *Wuthering Heights* finished and begins to make the round of publishers, along with *Agnes Grey* by Anne Brontë and *The Professor* by Charlotte; September 14, last dated complete poem.

1847   July, T. C. Newby accepts *Wuthering Heights* and *Agnes Grey,* but delays publishing until the success of *Jane Eyre* arouses interest in the "Bells"; December, *Wuthering Heights* and *Agnes Grey* published.

1848   Confusion in the literary world over the identity and number of the Bells; Anne publishes *The Tenant of Wildfell Hall*; Emily withdraws more resolutely into herself; September 24, Branwell dies; October 1, Emily leaves home for the last time to attend Branwell's funeral service—catches a severe cold which develops into inflammation of the lungs; December 19, Emily Brontë dies.

1850   *Wuthering Heights* reissued, with a selection of poems, and a biographical notice by Charlotte.

1893   The Brontë Society established.

1941   Hatfield's edition of *The Complete Poems of Emily Jane Brontë* published.

Chapter One

The Life of Emily Brontë

In his old age, after all his children were dead, the Rev. Patrick Brontë recalled an experiment he had made very early in their lives to encourage them to speak more openly. "I deemed that if they were put under a sort of cover I might gain my end," he said, "and happening to have a mask in the house, I told them all to stand and speak boldly from under cover of the mask." He then questioned them in turn, beginning with the youngest, Anne, "and asked what a child like her most wanted; she answered, 'Age and experience.'" He asked Emily what he should do "with her brother Branwell, who was sometimes a naughty boy; she answered, 'Reason with him, and when he won't listen to reason, whip him.'"[1] And so on through the other four. The answers are unexceptional, and what we might expect from children growing up to the strict catechism of the early nineteenth century. More significant is the image of the Brontës learning to express themselves from behind a mask. Although three of them were to develop remarkable and original gifts of expression, they never felt comfortable or capable in the outside world, without a cover to shield them from its direct glance. For years they wrote in secret and from the point of view of imaginary persons; when they published, it was under the mask of a pseudonym: Currer, Ellis, and Acton Bell. Charlotte and Anne took off the mask when it became necessary to appear in their own persons, but nothing could induce Emily to do so. When she died, the literary world was still engaged in the mystery of who was Ellis Bell.

The curiosity and speculations of the literary world did not interest Emily. Few writers have been as resolute as she was in not revealing herself. Only three of her letters have survived, and they tell nothing about her inner thoughts or feelings. She made no friends, and lived almost entirely at home. The time that she spent in school and her nine months in Brussels made no observable impression on her, whereas the same experiences occupy dozens of Charlotte's letters. Emily was virtually a self-contained being: what influenced her came from forces inside her, rather than from the outside, and it is no wonder that she struck those who knew her as being extremely reserved.

This was her impression on Ellen Nussey, Charlotte's closest friend, who gives us the fullest description we have of Emily's person, when she was about eighteen: "Emily Brontë had by this time acquired a lithe-some, graceful figure. She was the tallest person in the house, except for her father. Her hair, which was naturally as beautiful as Charlotte's, was in the same unbecoming tight curl and frizz, and there was the same want of complexion. She had very beautiful eyes—kind, kindling, liquid eyes; but she did not often look at you: she was too reserved. Their color might be said to be dark gray, at other times dark blue, they varied so. She talked very little."[2] In fact, Emily never talked very much.

When *Wuthering Heights* appeared, critics assumed it was the work of a man: it was too violent to be a woman's. Later her readers wondered how an inexperienced, retiring spinster, in a remote Anglican parson-age, could have conceived of and made so vivid the passion and fury of Catherine and Heathcliff. Her writings have been used to explain her life, and her life has been explored to interpret her writings. Yet although she lived and wrote with equal intensity, she kept an aesthetic distance between herself and her art, and we cannot turn with confi-dence to her poems and novel to fill in the gaps of her biographical record. This is not to say that her life and art do not reflect each other. As the housekeeper of Haworth and a visionary, she was and she wrote only what her nature required of her. How she traversed her separate realms without being divided by them, and why, at the end, the will or the ability to continue left her, we have now learned to accept that we will never entirely know. Who Emily Brontë was remains essentially a mystery—and one that continues to attract the solutions it eludes.

Background and Early Childhood

Emily Brontë was born at her father's parsonage in Thornton, near Bradford, in Yorkshire, on July 30, 1818, the fifth of six children born to Patrick Brontë and Maria Branwell in seven years. In April 1820, the family moved eight miles to the village of Haworth, where Mr. Brontë had been appointed curate for life. Situated near the great manufactur-ing towns of the West Riding, Haworth is built against a steep hill which is crossed by a narrow road that rises sharply from the cottages at the bottom to the Brontë residence on top. Behind the town, extending from the Brontës' garden are the stark, empty moors that Emily wandered in all seasons and loved with a special intensity. It was on the moors, Ellen Nussey says, that Emily dropped her reserve: "In fine and suitable weather delightful rambles were made over the moors, and down into the glens and ravines that here and there broke the monotony of the moorland. The rugged bank and rippling brook were treasures of delight. Emily, Anne, and Branwell used to ford the streams, and sometimes place stepping-stones for the other two; there was always a lingering delight in these spots,—every moss, every flower, every tint and form, were noted and enjoyed. Emily especially had a gleesome delight in these nooks of beauty,—her reserve for the time vanished." At their favorite spot, called "The Meeting of the Waters," Emily would play "like a young child with the tadpoles in the water, making them swim about . . . moralizing on the strong and the weak, the brave and the cowardly, as she chased them with her hand."[3] There was a timelessness about the moors that enabled Emily, even when grown up, to retain the freedom and intensity of her childhood. Mortality lay closer to home. Sanitary conditions in Haworth were primitive, and the graveyard of the church ran up to the wall of the Brontë house.

Emily Brontë's association with the Yorkshire moors is so strong that one tends to forget that the Brontës were not of Yorkshire stock, had no roots there, and in fact were aliens or strangers. Maria Branwell came from Penzance, in Cornwall, far to the south, where there are palm trees and mild winters. Her family was Methodist and middle-class. A gentle, independent woman, she married Patrick Brontë in 1812, when she was twenty-nine years old. The father of the Brontës was born in Ireland, in 1777, of poor and probably illiterate parents. Ambitious and persevering, he acquired an education, taught school in Ireland, and in 1802 he entered Cambridge. After graduation and ordination in the Church of England, his various ministries took him eventually to Yorkshire, where he met Maria Branwell. In 1811, he published the first of his four books of poetry and fiction, *Cottage Poems*.[4] In middle age Patrick Brontë became an eccentric, strong-willed man—he carried regularly a loaded gun on his person—but he was not the tyrant portrayed by Mrs. Gaskell, who says that on one occasion he burned his children's colored boots because they were too luxurious.[5] He loved his children, encouraged their interest in literature, and gave them the free choice of his library. The children devoured Aesop and the *Arabian Nights* as well as the modern Romantic writers, especially Scott and Byron. They derived from their father as well a strong interest in contemporary politics. As young children the Brontës read *Blackwood's Magazine,* their favorite periodical, Whig and Tory newspapers, and in 1829 they were eagerly discussing the question of Catholic emancipation.

Emily never knew her mother. Mrs. Brontë contracted internal cancer shortly after the family's removal to Haworth, confined herself to her room, and died in September 1821, when Emily was three years old. Elizabeth Branwell, Mrs. Brontë's sister, who had tended her in her illness, came to live at the parsonage and instructed her nieces in the principles of orderly housekeeping. But she did not become a second mother to them; that office fell to the oldest of the Brontë children, Maria, then eight years old. Apparently a brilliant child, and the original of Helen Burns in *Jane Eyre,* Maria gathered her brother and sisters in a small room on the second floor, and kept them entertained and quiet for hours, while she read the parliamentary debates from the papers. With no contacts outside their home, and separated for long periods of the day from their father and aunt, the young Brontës formed a vital, self-contained group among themselves.

Knowing that his daughters would need an education for the day when they would have to support themselves, in July 1824, Mr. Brontë took Maria and the next eldest, Elizabeth, to the Clergy Daughters' School at Cowan Bridge. Charlotte followed them in August, and Emily in November. What happened at Cowan Bridge, the Lowood of *Jane Eyre,* in the winter and spring of 1825, is still a controversy. When they left home, the two older girls were still recovering from the effects of whooping cough. At Cowan Bridge, they were subjected to privation and strict discipline, and even before the typhoid epidemic broke out in April, Maria had been taken home by her father, critically ill from consumption. The girl who had taken the place of Emily's mother died on May 6. Almost immediately afterwards, Elizabeth was sent home with the same illness, and died June 15. Mr. Brontë had already brought Charlotte and Emily home. Her sisters' deaths haunted Charlotte for years; on Emily the effect was unconscious, but perhaps just as lasting. Coming to self-consciousness in the midst of so much sickness and death, she learned to depend entirely on her own powers and to trust to her own sense of permanence.

The Group Plays and the Creation of Gondal

In June 1826, Mr. Brontë returned home late from a visit to Leeds, with presents for his children, including a box of wooden soldiers for Branwell. The next morning marked a turning point in their lives. As Charlotte describes it, when Branwell came to the room where she and Emily slept, to show them the soldiers, the girls jumped out of bed and, Charlotte says, "I snatched up one and exclaimed: 'This is the Duke of Wellington! This shall be the Duke.' When I had said this Emily likewise took up one and said it should be hers; when Anne came down, she said one should be hers. . . . Emily's was a grave-looking fellow, and we called him 'Gravey.' Anne's was a queer little thing, much like herself, and we called him 'Waiting-Boy.' Branwell chose his and called him Bounaparte."[6] Transformed into characters, the soldiers became dramatis personae in an imaginative venture that would occupy Charlotte for more than a decade, and Branwell, Emily, and Anne for the better part of their lives. What we now know as the Brontë juvenilia—the long record of apprenticeship composition preceding the Brontës' appearance in print—had begun.

It began as an oral literature. The Brontës made up plays based on the lives of the toy soldiers, whom they called the Young Men, and acted the parts themselves. They performed with such energy that once they frightened their elderly servant, Tabby, out of the house. She went to her nephew's and begged him to go to the parsonage, because she was sure the children were going mad, and she dare not stay in the house with them. "When the nephew reached the parsonage, 'the childer set up a great crack o' laughin',' at the wonderful joke they had perpetrated on faithful Tabby."[7] Their plays went through three major cycles. After a year, the Young Men's Play ended, and they began a new game, called Our Fellows, "in which each child had as his own a large island inhabited by people six miles high. . . ."[8] In December 1827, they began the play of the Islanders, in which each child took an actual island and peopled it with his or her favorite heroes. "These," Charlotte says, "are our three great plays that are not kept secret." She and Emily made up secret plays as well, lying together in bed, before they went to sleep.[9] Influenced by the *Arabian Nights,* the children thought of themselves as genii—Chief Genius Tallii, Brannii, Emmii, and Annii they called themselves—who oversaw the adventures of their heroes with omnipotent power over life and death.

In 1829, the Brontës returned to the original twelve wooden solders and sent them on an expedition to the northwest coast of Africa, which they explored and conquered and called the Glasstown Confederacy. To record the exploits of the soldiers, Branwell put together a miniature *Blackwood's Magazine,* which Fanny Ratchford describes as "a tiny periodical of four leaves measuring about 2½ x 1½ inches, proportionate in size, as he calculated, to his wooden soldiers." Branwell wrote in as small a hand as he could contrive, to approximate the handwriting of a toy soldier—and possibly because paper would not be plentiful at the parsonage. All of the Brontës learned to write in the same minute hand, by which they could cover a small page with hundreds of words and keep their writing secret—later a consideration of great importance to Emily. Even their father did not know of their accomplishment until nearly two decades later, when Charlotte presented him with a published copy of *Jane Eyre.* The first issue of Branwell's magazine contained a scientific article, poetry, and "an account of the author's voyage to Mons Island from Glass Town." The two articles were illustrated.[10] Charlotte quickly realized the creative possibilities of the magazine and began to contribute to it. The Brontës' written literature had begun.

Emily and Anne took an active part in the Glass Town story, and their chief men—now named Parry and Ross—had lands named for them in the Confederacy, but they probably did not write for it. They were necessarily subordinate to the older and prolific Charlotte and Branwell, and in time felt the need for their own creation. When Charlotte left home for Roe Head School in January 1831, leaving Branwell in charge of the play, Emily and Anne defected and began a fantasy literature of their own—a saga centered on an imaginary island in the north Pacific, called Gondal. Henceforth, the four were divided into pairs writing independently of each other, although there are parallel lines of development between the Gondal and the Glass Town (later Angrian) stories. Emily shared her Gondal thoughts and writing only with Anne.

Gondal appears in the earliest piece of writing from Brontë that we have, a diary entry dated November 24, 1834, when she was sixteen years old.

Taby said just now Come Anne pilloputate (i.e. pill a potato) Aunt has come into the kitchen just now and said where are you feet Anne Anne answered On the floor Aunt papa opened the parlour door and gave Branwell a letter saying here Branwell read this and show it to your Aunt and Charlotte—The Gondals are discovering the interior of Gaaldine Sally Mosley is washing in the back kitchen

It is past Twelve o'clock Anne and I have not tidied ourselves, done our bedwork or done our lessons and we want to go out to play we are going to have for Dinner Boiled Beef, Turnips, potatoes and applepudding. The Kitchin is in a very untidy state Anne and I have not done our music exercise which consists of b major Taby said on my putting a pen in her face Ya pitter pottering there instead of pilling a potate I answered O Dear, O Dear, O dear I will directly with that I get up, take a knife and begin pilling (finished pilling the potatoes)[11]

Despite the imperfect grammar, the kitchen scene and a slice of Brontë's life are brought into sharp focus. Like typical teenagers, Anne and Emily postpone their lessons and chores until the last minute, and are not very intimidated by the supervising adults. They are still considered children, apparently, not privileged to read the letter which goes to Branwell, Charlotte, and their aunt. Although money was scarce at the parsonage—the girls could not always afford postage for their letters—the family ate well. Finally, Brontë makes no distinction between the imaginary and the factual worlds: the Gondals are discovering the interior of Gaaldine while Sally Mosley washes in the back kitchen. The two events are equally present to her as she peels potatoes at the kitchen table.

Brontë is noting down the stage which she and Anne have reached in the Gondal story. Gondal explorers have begun to colonize Gaaldine, an island in the south Pacific. The story was almost certainly still being told between them, rather than written—we do not know when Brontë's creative writing began. Her earliest dated poem in Hatfield's definitive edition is July 12, 1836.[12] In any event, the oral literature which she shared with Anne would have had to come to an abrupt halt in 1835—forcing her, if force was necessary, to turn to her writing desk.

The Reluctant Scholar

When Charlotte returned from Roe Head School in 1832, she taught her two sisters what she had learned in history, grammar, geography, drawing, and French. The next three years passed pleasantly for all.

Despite the necessity of peeling potatoes and practicing the piano, Brontë had ample time to do as she liked—moreover, she enjoyed and was good at her housekeeping and her music. "An account of one day is an account of all," Charlotte writes. "In the mornings, from 9 o'clock to half-past 12, I instruct my sisters and draw, then we walk till dinner, after dinner I sew till tea-time, and after tea I either read, write, do a little fancy work, or draw, as I please. Thus in one delightful, though somewhat monotonous course, my life is passed."[13] Emily would have spent her day in much the same way, except that the routine of her home was not monotonous to her. It was only at home that she found the measure of freedom and the emotional ballast she required. Since Cowan Bridge, she had remained at home, although she was now past the age at which Charlotte went to Roe Head. And it was Charlotte who now began to think, not only of her own livelihood in the future, but of Emily's.

In July 1835, Charlotte obtained a teaching position at Roe Head School, with terms that included the free education of one of her sisters. Emily, the next in line, was persuaded to take advantage of the opportunity. Mr. Brontë was now almost sixty years old and not in robust health. When he died, the Brontës would have to provide for themselves, and even their home would no longer be theirs. Women of their time and station had very limited opportunities to earn a living, outside of teaching; income and advancement as a teacher or governess depended on one's training and credentials. The Brontë sisters could not look to their father to support their education. The little that he could spare from his income was to go to Branwell, who in the same summer was making plans to enter the Royal Academy for Artists in London. The Brontës never enjoyed teaching, or submitting themselves to another's regulations, and they did not like or feel comfortable with children. Later, when she was teaching at Law Hill, Brontë is reported to have told her students that she preferred the company of the school's dogs to theirs.[14] Yet there was no alternative but to go to Roe Head.

The change almost killed her. Although Roe Head is less than twenty miles from Haworth and only four from the home of Charlotte's friend, Ellen Nussey, and although Charlotte was with her, Emily became severely ill from homesickness. Years later, in her Preface to Emily's poems, Charlotte recalls the episode and the alarm she felt at watching her sister decline:

Liberty was the breath of Emily's nostrils; without it, she perished. The change from her own home to a school, and from her own very noiseless, very secluded, but unrestricted and inartificial mode of life, to one of disciplined routine (though under the kindliest auspices) was what she failed in enduring. Her nature proved here too strong for her fortitude. Every morning when she woke, the vision of home and the moors rushed on her, and darkened and saddened the day that lay before her. Nobody knew what ailed her but me—I knew only too well. In this struggle her health was quickly broken: her white face, attenuated form, and failing strength threatened rapid decline. I felt in my heart she would die, if she did not go home, and with this conviction obtained her recall.[15]

After only three months Emily returned home to assist in the housekeeping with her father, her aunt, and Tabby, while Anne took her place at Roe Head.

"Liberty was the breath of Emily's nostrils": almost everyone who has written about Brontë, since Charlotte, agrees. She could survive and even flourish in the absence of her beloved Anne, but not without the freedom to range the moors and, more crucially, not without Gondal. The discipline at Roe Head was not harsh or demanding, but it drove a wedge between her and her imaginative life. Charlotte knew this, as she says, "only too well." Her own letters from Roe Head reflect the inner torment she suffered at having to suppress her urgent desire to write. But whereas Charlotte had a strong sense of duty to sustain her in her uncongenial work, Emily did not. One of her poems, although it was written later, when she had been a teacher as well as a student, almost certainly expresses her feelings about Roe Head:

> A little while, a little while,
> The noisy crowd are barred away;
> And I can sing and I can smile
> A little while I've holyday!
>
> Where wilt thou go, my harassed heart?
> Full many a land invites thee now;
> And places near and far apart
> Have rest for thee, my weary brow.

Both the familiar moors of her home and the landscape of Gondal appear to her, but the freedom to indulge in her vision is cut short:

I hear my dungeon bars recoil—

Even as I stood with raptured eye
Absorbed in bliss so deep and dear
My hour of rest had fleeted by
And given me back to weary care.[16]

The school room is her imagination's prison.

Brontë spent the two years after Roe Head educating herself, as well as assuming a major share of the household work. There is a firmly established tradition that she studied German from a book propped in front of her, while she made the family's bread. The excellence of her bread is likewise widely accepted. During the Christmas holidays of 1836, when all of the sisters were together, the servant Tabby fell in an icy street and broke her leg. When Aunt Branwell wanted Tabby removed to her sister's cottage to save the trouble of caring for her at the parsonage, the three Brontës rebelled. Tabby was one of the family to them, had cared for them in their childhood, and they would now nurse her. They went on a hunger strike, refusing to touch their meals until they had won. When Charlotte and Anne returned to Roe Head, all of the household chores that had been Tabby's would fall, in addition to her own, on Emily. And as Gérin reminds us, "At a time when all the household bread was baked at home, and the heavy domestic washing was a weekly event in the out-house . . . Emily's task was a heavy one."[17] On the other hand, from the talkative old Yorkshire servant sitting in the kitchen with her, speaking the local dialect, Brontë's ear picked up the rhythm and sound of a direct expressive speech, and she stored away numerous anecdotes and legends of the surrounding area.

In the diary paper which Emily and Anne wrote on June 26, 1837, we find them living, with much contentment, a busy, satisfying life. A Gondal coronation is being planned to parallel Queen Victoria's, and the two girls are at least keeping up with events in Angria, as the reference to Charlotte's and Branwell's heroes—Zamorna and Northangerland—show. Augusta Almeda, whose life Emily is writing, is the heroine of her own Gondal poems. It is "Monday evening June 26 1837":

A bit past 4 o'clock Charlotte working in Aunt's room, Branwell reading Eugene Aram to her—Anne and I writing in the drawing-room—Anne a poem beginning "Fair was the evening and brightly the sun"—I Augusta Almeda's life 1st v. 1-4th page from the last—fine rather coolish thin grey cloudy but sunny day Aunt working in the little room the old nursery Papa gone out Tabby in the kitchen—The Emperors and Empresses of Gondal and Gaaldine preparing to depart from Gaaldine to prepare for the coronation which will be on the 12th July Queen Vittoria ascended the throne this month. Northangerland in Monkey's Isle—Zamorna at Eversham. All tight and right in which condition it is to be hoped we shall be at this day 4 years at which time Charlotte will be 25 and 2 months—Branwell just 24 it being his birthday—myself 22 and 10 months and a piece Anne 21 and nearly a half I wonder where we shall be and how we shall be and what kind of a day it will be then—let us hope for the best[18]

As in the note of 1834, Brontë moves freely between everyday household affairs and the imaginary events of Gondal. She is fully recovered from the experience at Roe Head, and says nothing to suggest that life at the parsonage that summer was anything but agreeable to her.

It comes as a surprise, therefore, to find her going off as a teacher in Law Hill School several months later. The decision probably perplexed Charlotte as well, who wrote to Ellen Nussey on October 2, 1837, "My sister Emily is gone into a situation as teacher in a large school of near forty pupils, near Halifax. I have had one letter from her since her departure; it gives an appalling account of her duties—hard labour from six in the morning until near eleven at night, with only one half-hour of exercise between. This is slavery. I fear she will never stand it."[19] We know practically nothing else about Brontë's stay at Law Hill, which, according to Gérin, lasted from September 1837 to the following spring.[20] Estimates among the authorities vary, however, from six months to two and a half years—from September 1836, that is, to May 1839.

We can only guess why Brontë left the happy life she describes at home for the slavery she describes to Charlotte. The Brontës' need to support themselves was as pressing as ever. Charlotte, the only one of the sisters earning a salary, was not able to save any of it. And the family's chief hope, Branwell, had proved an utter disappointment. When Emily returned from Roe Head in the fall of 1835, she found Branwell back from London: the Royal Academy venture had come to nothing. Without ever approaching the Academy, Branwell spent in a local pub the money given him for his studies. As failures, Branwell and

Emily found refuge in each other; they saw themselves as outcasts or misfits in a success-oriented society, and in later years, when Branwell became a complete wreck, Emily's attitude toward him remained the most tolerant and understanding of the family. Moreover, Branwell's primary passion, like Emily's, was for literature; he wanted a writing career, and wrote to *Blackwood's* offering his services. His hopes and plans for the future, his excited recitals of the Angrian epic, are what probably stimulated Emily to begin writing the Gondal story that she and Anne had been telling.

It was, perhaps, too pleasant and easy to remain at home while her sisters made all the sacrifices. And although Emily never showed much concern about money or the future, her conscience—the feeling that she should be doing her part too—led her to accept the position at Law Hill after Charlotte and Anne had returned to Roe Head. Once over her initial difficulties—Brontë probably never adjusted fully to the demands and the routine of teaching—the situation of the school and its view of the surrounding heaths would have pleased her. Leyland says that she could see Roe Head, where her sisters were, and almost as far as home.[21] Daily contact with her students and close interaction with her mistress, Elizabeth Patchett, expanded her knowledge of human nature. Chadwick suggests that the structure and immediate surroundings of Law Hill School are the model for Wuthering Heights.[22] The history of the building, which concerns the rise of an unscrupulous orphan over his adopted family's home and fortunes, has parallels with the story of Heathcliff among the Earnshaws.[23]

Undoubtedly, Brontë exaggerated when she wrote to Charlotte, and did have more than one half-hour free from her duties to write and reflect. Hatfield places thirty of her poems between September 30, 1837, and May 1838. Some of these may have been written or begun during the Christmas vacation—the dates she appended to her poems sometimes stand for the day of the first draft, sometimes for that of the final copy; other poems, such as "A little while, a little while," may have been begun at Law Hill and finished later. Nonetheless, her teaching duties did not check her creative output. Indeed, her artistic power was growing, and so was her special vision, which can only be called "mystical," and which found expression in a poem of February 1838:

I'm happiest when most away
I can bear my soul from its home of clay
On a windy night when the moon is bright
And the eye can wander through worlds of light—

When I am not and none beside—
Nor earth nor sea nor cloudless sky—
But only spirit wandering wide
Through infinite immensity.[24]

It is from such poems as these, expressing her sense of oneness with a transcendent over-soul, that we get a sense of her religion.

Brontë's return home from Law Hill, in May or June of 1838, coincided with Charlotte's from Roe Head, and the three sisters were together until Anne left to be a private governess the following April. The period is one of Brontë's most creative: the Gondal saga was growing, and by the time of her twenty-second birthday in 1840, she had written well over two-thirds of her known verse. Outwardly, her life passed uneventfully; inwardly, she created new speakers for her poems, expanded her themes of captivity and prisonhood, and identified herself with the figure of the wanderer and exile. Her earliest biographer, Mary Robinson, was the first to project the image of two Emily Brontës: "Two lives went on side by side in her heart, neither ever mingling with or interrupting the other. Practical housewife with capable hands, dreamer of strange horrors; each self was independent of the companion to which it was linked by day and night."[25] Although she wrote powerfully about love and sexual attraction, there is no evidence that she ever had a lover or desired one. In 1839, a new curate, William Weightman, came to live opposite the parsonage. Likable and young, Weightman attracted Anne and flirted with Ellen Nussey when she came to visit. Brontë decided that he needed watching and appointed herself Ellen's bodyguard on their outings, earning for herself the nickname of The Major. Robinson, who obtained some of her information from Ellen Nussey, says that when curates came looking for Mr. Brontë in his study, they occasionally found Emily there instead, and "used to beat such a hasty retreat that it was quite an established joke at the Parsonage that Emily appeared to the outer world in the likeness of an old bear. She hated strange faces and strange places. Her sisters must have seen that such a temperament, if it made her unlikely to attract a husband or wish to attract one, also rendered her lamentably unfit to earn her living as a governess. In those days they could not tell that the defect was incurable, a congenital infirmity of nature."[26] Yet the impression Brontë leaves is one of strength and self-acceptance. She had none of the religious melancholia that troubled Anne. And the division between her domestic and imaginative selves did not torment her as it did Charlotte.

Brontë's strength could be awesome. She loved animals and took charge of the family's pets, which at one time included a hawk. Her favorite was Keeper, a large, fierce dog, unmanageable with anyone else but devoted to her. Her aunt objected to Keeper's being in the house because it would lie on the beds and soil the sheets. Brontë promised to stop that, and catching Keeper stretched on one of their beds, she dragged him down the stairs by main force, the dog growling savagely. There was no time to fetch a stick, lest the dog spring at her throat, so she beat its muzzle with her bare fists until its face was swollen. Immediately, she nursed the wounds. On another occasion, she offered water to a strange dog in the street, and it bit her. She went into the kitchen, took a red hot iron from the fire, and pressed it on the wound—telling no one of the incident until the danger of rabies was over.[27]

The School Plan and Brussels

In her third diary paper, written July 30, 1841, Brontë announces her and her sisters' plan to establish a school of their own: ". . . as yet nothing is determined, but I hope and trust it may go on and prosper and answer our highest expectations. This day four years I wonder whether we shall still be dragging on in our present condition or established to our heart's content." She pictures them "merrily seated" in their "own sitting-room in some pleasant and flourishing seminary," their debts paid off, and their father, aunt, and Branwell either just arriving for a visit or having just left. "It will be a fine warm summer evening, very different from this bleak look-out, and Anne and I will perchance slip out into the garden for a few minutes to peruse our papers. I hope either this or something better will be the case."[28] Although dissatisfied and "dragging on," Brontë is not despondent. She is eager and sanguine about the school project; for herself and her writing, she says she has a good many books on hand, and resolves to do great things. But she was home alone, with her father and her aunt; Charlotte, Branwell, and Anne had again dispersed to separate places of employment; and the sisters were rebelling against the enforced separation from each other imposed by teaching and governessing for strangers. They thought that a school of their own, although it would probably be away from Haworth, would keep them together and give them the security and mental freedom they desired.

Charlotte became convinced that she and her sisters would have a better chance of success if they obtained more schooling themselves— preferably on the Continent, where living expenses were cheaper than in England, and where they could advance their study of foreign languages. Charlotte persuaded their aunt to lend them money, and throughout the fall of 1841, inquiries were made respecting schools in Belgium and France. Brontë seems to have been troubled by the decision to have Anne remain as governess with the Robinson family at Thorp Green, for Charlotte wrote to her on November 7, 1841: "Anne seems omitted in the present plan, but if all goes right I trust she will derive her full share of benefit from it in the end. I exhort all to hope. I believe in my heart this is acting for the best; my only fear is lest others should doubt and be dismayed."[29] Neither Charlotte nor Emily had ever been outside of Yorkshire or the neighboring counties, and Emily's experiences away from home had not been happy ones. But she offered no objection, and on February 8, 1842, the two Brontës, accompanied by their father, went to London; on the twelfth; they sailed for Ostend.[30] They had decided, at almost the last minute, upon a school for young ladies in Brussels, the Pensionnat Héger.

Brontë went to Brussels to study, and study she did. Otherwise, the experience, which was to be a major influence on Charlotte, seems hardly to have touched her. She had a much greater language difficulty to overcome than Charlotte, who said that Emily had to work "like a horse." In their twenties, the Brontës were older than the other students, and felt isolated from students and teachers by their nationality and religion. "All in the house are Catholics except ourselves, one

other girl, and the gouvernante of Madame's children," Charlotte wrote
Ellen Nussey. "The difference in country and religion makes a broad
line of demarcation between us and all the rest. We are completely
isolated in the midst of numbers."[31] Brontë's withdrawal into her
studies was almost total. On Sundays and holidays, the sisters could
visit Charlotte's friends, the Taylors, just outside of Brussels, or cousins
of the Taylors in town, but their shyness remained overpowering. The
wife of an English clergyman in Brussels, Mrs. Jenkins, told Elizabeth
Gaskell that "she used to ask them to spend Sundays and holidays with
her, until she found that they felt more pain than pleasure from such
visits. Emily hardly ever uttered more than a monosyllable," and before
Charlotte could bring herself to speak, she would turn in her chair so as
to hide her face from the person she was speaking to.[32]

Yet Brontë made progress. The essays in French which she wrote for
M. Héger show her grappling with moral and philosophical problems
in a direct and an individual way. Héger would read the Brontës
selections from the French masters and then ask them to express their
own ideas in a similar style. Brontë, who did not get along with Héger,
objected to the method as one which would cause them to "lose all
originality of thought and expression."[33] Héger, on the other hand, at
least when he was speaking to Mrs. Gaskell after the death of Charlotte,
remembered Emily for her strength and tenacity of purpose. "She
should have been a man—a great navigator," he said. "Her powerful
reason would have deduced new spheres of discovery from the knowledge of the old; and her strong, imperious will would never have been
daunted by opposition or difficulty; never have given way but with
life." The power of her imagination was such that, had she written a
history, it would have forced the reader to accept its perception of the
truth. Then, reversing the usual roles in which we find the sisters, in
which Charlotte is always the prime mover, he commented that Emily
"appeared egotistical and exacting compared to Charlotte, who was
always unselfish . . . and in the anxiety of the elder to make her
younger sister contented, she allowed her to exercise a kind of unconscious tyranny over her."[34] Both had impressed the Hégers, and in the
summer of 1842, Madame Héger proposed to them that they remain at
the Pensionnat another half year as student teachers. No salary was
offered, only their board and tuition, but the offer represented a move
forward in the direction they hoped to take. Thus, Charlotte agreed to

teach English, and Emily, now a skilled musician, began to give lessons on the piano.

The new term had just begun, however, when news reached them, on November 2, 1842, that their aunt was gravely ill. The next morning they learned that she had died on October 29. Although neither Emily nor Charlotte was emotionally attached to their aunt, they respected her and had lived with her for twenty years. They immediately made preparations to leave, and arrived home on November 8, having been in Belgium nine months.[35] Aunt Branwell had been frugal and saving, and in her will she left each of the Brontë sisters 350 pounds. It was the first time they had any money of their own beyond their meager earnings as governess or teacher.

A Short, Happy Life

One of the sisters would now have to remain at home to look after their father, and it is unlikely, even without the inheritance, that Brontë ever intended to return to Brussels. After the others had left, the responsibility of investing their inheritance fell, as Gérin says, "ironically enough, on Emily, who had never given money a thought."[36] She proved herself, however, more than capable of handling business matters. She was now in charge of the house, and spent the greater part of 1843 alone with Tabby and her father who, according to a local legend, taught her to shoot his pistols, in case she should have to defend their property. She would fire the gun, then run into the kitchen to roll out a tray of tea-cakes; wiping her hands, she returned to her father in the garden for another round of practice. She reportedly became an expert shot.[37] And there were long afternoons spent wandering the moors, when she would lie on a bank of heath, watching the clouds cross the sky and writing poetry. When Charlotte returned from Brussels at the beginning of 1844, shattered after a year of inner conflict, loneliness, and neglect, Brontë restored her to health by taking her for long walks on the Haworth moors.

Charlotte still hoped to have a school of their own, and the sisters sent out a printed advertisement of "The Misses Brontë's Establishment for the Board and Education of a Limited Number of Young Ladies." No students ever applied, though their efforts to secure one dragged on for a year. Emily was no longer enthusiastic about the project, and gave it up easily. She felt that their aunt's money was enough for their needs, and that she was free to direct her attention where she pleased. In February 1844, she began to select and arrange her manuscript poems into two notebooks: one containing forty-five poems and titled "Gondal Poems"; the other, untitled, containing thirty-one poems. Although in the next year and a half her output was small, it includes some of her best poems. The Gondal story was now fully developed in her mind, and her birthday note of July 30, 1845, shows that she has kept all of her youthful enthusiasm for it. In June, she and Anne had taken their first overnight journey together, and while traveling they pretended to be various Gondal heroes and heroines:

Anne and I went our first long journey by ourselves together, leaving home on the 30th of June, Monday, sleeping at York, returning to Keighley Tuesday evening, sleeping there and walking home on Wednesday morning. Though the weather was broken we enjoyed ourselves very much, except during a few hours at Bradford. And during our excursion we were, Ronald Macalgin, Henry Angora, Juliet Augusteena, Rosabella Esmaldan, Ella and Julian Egremont, Catherine Navarre, and Cordelia Fitzaphnold, escaping from the palaces of instruction to join the Royalists who are hard driven at present by the victorious Republicans. The Gondals still flourish bright as ever. I am at present writing a work on the First War. Anne has been writing some articles on this, and a book by Henry Sophona. We intend sticking firm by the rascals as long as they delight us, which I am glad to say they do at present.[38]

Essentially, Brontë has not changed at all; at twenty-seven she is still playing the game that began with the wooden soldiers when she was eight. In contrast, Anne has grown tired of the Gondals, and in her companion note to Emily's, she says wearily of the Gondal chronicles, "When will they be done? . . . The Gondals in general are not in a first-rate playing condition. Will they improve?"[39]

Anne had been shocked by the conduct of her brother and the wife of her employer at Thorp Green—she had quit her job and Branwell had been fired after what was most probably an adulterous affair. Charlotte, who had fallen in love with M. Héger, was suffering from a passion she could neither acknowledge nor control. Emily, on the other hand, the most reserved and the least social of the family, was full of animal spirits and cheer: "I am quite contented for myself: not as idle as formerly, altogether as hearty, and having learnt to make the most of the present and long for the future with the fidgetiness that I cannot do all I wish; seldom or ever troubled with nothing to do, and merely desiring that everybody could be as comfortable as myself and as undesponding, and then we should have a very tolerable world of it." She has to close her note because she has ironing to do. Besides, "I have plenty of work on hand, and writing, and am altogether full of business."[40] It is possible, though not likely, that she had already begun *Wuthering Heights*; at the latest, she was writing the novel within six months of the July 30 note. Yet nothing seems farther from the cheerful tone and optimism with which she describes her life in the summer of 1845 than the dark brooding and bitter resentment of her most famous work. An explanation, of course, is that Brontë had been playing at being other people for twenty years, and perfected the technique in her novel.

Having the companionship of her sisters and the freedom to pursue her deepest interests, Brontë did not want her life to change. But one day in October, she left her poetry notebook on her desk, where Charlotte found it. As she read, Charlotte says, "something more than surprize seized me,—a deep conviction that these were not common effusions, nor at all like the poetry women generally write. I thought them condensed and terse, vigorous and genuine. To my ear, they had also a peculiar music—wild, melancholy, and elevating."[41] Charlotte knew at once that the poems ought to be published, but Emily exploded with anger at the intrusion, and a fierce scene ensued. Emily valued her privacy highly, and the interference of anyone, even her sister's, with her imaginative life threatened the equilibrium she had always maintained between her inner and her outer worlds. It took hours to reconcile her to the discovery of the poems, and days to persuade her to publish them. Anne sided with Charlotte and produced poems of her own, as did Charlotte. For her sisters there was no turning back, and Emily could not oppose them without wounding them. The Brontës decided not to send their manuscript out under their real names, because they feared that, as women writers, they would not be fairly treated. But they did not want to pose positively as men either. They chose pseudonyms that would not identify their sex, and the Brontës became Currer, Ellis, and Acton Bell.

They did not know how or where to submit their manuscript, and wrote to Chambers of Edinburgh for advice about the likely prospects for a book of poems. A publisher, the London firm of Aylott and Jones, accepted the poems in January 1846, after the Brontës agreed to pay the costs of publication. All of the correspondence with Aylott and Jones was conducted by Charlotte, writing as Currer Bell. Emily's feelings about the book were ambivalent. She had to change the Gondal references in her poems to make them intelligible to the reader, and thus violate the purpose for which she wrote them. "To a girl with so reticent a nature," as Winifred Gérin remarks, "the revelation of her most secret experiences was wholly repugnant. Poems, whose existence she had never mentioned to Charlotte and barely mentioned to Anne, were now to be exposed to the judgment of strangers."[42] Yet it is difficult to believe that she was indifferent to the fate of the book, or that she was unaffected by Charlotte's excitement over the reality of what had been a long-cherished dream of authorship. Their brief lives as public writers was one of the happiest times the Brontës knew.

Poems by Currer, Ellis, and Acton Bell, containing nineteen poems by Charlotte and twenty-one each by Emily and Anne, was published and available for sale at the end of May, 1846. It had cost the Brontës well over the thirty-five pounds they had agreed to pay. It sold two copies—though one of the buyers was so struck by it that he wrote the Bells asking for their autographs. What mattered to the Brontës more than sales was that they had succeeded in getting into print, and that they were no longer "unknown" authors. Before the poems had been accepted—probably within weeks of Charlotte's discovery of Emily's notebook—the three were at work on their fiction. In April 1846, Charlotte wrote to Aylott and Jones to say that the Bells were "preparing for the press a work of fiction, consisting of three distinct and unconnected tales, which may be published either together, as a work of three volumes, of the ordinary novel size, or separately as single volumes, as shall be deemed most advisable."[43] This time, they did not intend to pay the costs themselves—although, as it turned out, Emily and Anne had to advance fifty pounds against the sale of 250 copies of their novels. It is from this spring of 1846—when Charlotte was writing *The Professor*; Emily, *Wuthering Heights*; and Anne, *Agnes Grey*—that we get one of the most enduring and moving scenes of their life together. Their work for the day done and put away, and the rest of the house asleep, the three sisters paced the sitting room, arms around each other's waist, comparing notes on their novels, and one of them reading to the others her latest chapter.[44] If nothing else, it refutes the notion that Emily allowed no one ever to enter the sanctuary of her thoughts. The ideal condition for herself and her sisters, which she had projected in the diary note of 1841, had virtually come to pass.

The Brontës finished their novels in July 1846 and submitted them to publishers, without success, for a year. As their envelope returned to them, with a curt, informal rejection slip, the Brontës innocently crossed out the name of the firm they had last sent their novels to and added on the same envelope the name of the next on their list. Finally, in July 1847, Thomas Newby offered to publish *Wuthering Heights* and *Agnes Grey,* but not *The Professor.* Besides the blow to Charlotte, this meant that Emily and Anne would have to conduct their literary business on their own, and with a man who did not hesitate to take advantage of their inexperience.

Newby's treatment of them was, at the least, dishonest. Although he had agreed to terms in July, and had sent the first proof sheets to Haworth in August, he delayed publication and ignored the Brontës' letters of inquiry. *Jane Eyre,* in the meanwhile, which was not finished until August 1847, was published by Smith Elder in October. It became an immediate best seller, and made the Messrs. Bell the focus of considerable interest and curiosity. Hoping to profit from the popularity of *Jane Eyre* and from the confusion about the identities of the Bells, Newby published *Wuthering Heights* and *Agnes Grey* in December, and helped to spread the rumor that all three novels were the work of one author. The books had a shabby appearance, and none of the corrections Emily made on the proof sheets appeared in print.[45] And though sales were moderately good, Newby did not refund the fifty pounds he had required as a guarantee against losses. Contrasting her own excellent treatment from Smith Elder, with that of her sisters, Charlotte assumed they were fed up with Newby, and she wrote to W. S. Williams, her publisher's reader, to intimate that Ellis and Action would not want to have Newby for their publisher a second time.

But she could no longer influence Emily. A rift was growing between the two—indeed, between Emily and the world outside her—that Charlotte could only look across in dismay. "It may be," as Muriel Spark suggests, "that Emily was, from 1847 onward, unbalanced in mind, and that this disaster fell more severely upon her during her last months."[46] We only know that after finishing *Wuthering Heights*

Brontë withdrew into herself, and ceased even to write. The notion that she was at work on a second novel before she died has never been substantiated, and for the crucial years of 1846–1848 we have only two of her poems. The publication of her writing had taken away the desire or the capacity to produce more—even though her work had already made an impact. The several reviews of the *Poems* picked Emily's as the most noteworthy of the three Bells. And although *Wuthering Heights* was generally misunderstood when it appeared, the general impression that it was uniformly condemned is not accurate: its power as well as its disagreeableness was noted. Reviews of her novel were found in Brontë's desk after her death, but to her mind these had to do with Ellis Bell, who had become a separate personage from Emily Brontë. After Charlotte and Anne had gone to London to prove to their publishers the separate identities and authorship of the Bells, Charlotte had to write Williams to warn him not to refer to her sisters in the plural. "Ellis Bell will not endure to be alluded to under any other appellation than the *nom de plume*. I committed a grand error in betraying his identity to you and Mr. Smith. It was inadvertent—the words 'we are three sisters' escaped me before I was aware. . . . I regret it bitterly now, for I find it is against every feeling and intention of Ellis Bell."[47] Apparently, there had been a scene similar to the one following Charlotte's discovery of the notebook. Having exposed herself once was enough: Emily Brontë retreated more resolutely than ever into her private world.

But even there she could find no sanctuary. The triumph and achievement of the Brontës' imagination smashed into the tragedy of their realities. In 1846, Mr. Brontë was almost blind with cataract, and Charlotte had to take him to Manchester for an eye operation. While there, she wondered "how poor Emily and Anne will get on at home with Branwell[.] They too will have their troubles."[48] Branwell's case was already hopeless. He had believed that Mrs. Robinson, at Thorp Green, fully returned his love and intended to marry him after the death of her ailing husband. Her plans, however, did not include Branwell at all, and she took the first opportunity after her husband's death to notify Branwell that they could never meet again. Branwell collapsed in a fit. Already a drunkard and addicted to opium, he became a constant spectral presence in the house, wretched when sober, insensible when he could borrow or connive money for drink or drugs.

Charlotte came to despise him, and references to Branwell in her letters, from the time of his dismissal from Thorp Green until his death, are almost always contemptuous. Following Mary Robinson, on the other hand, Brontë biographers have presented Emily as Branwell's advocate or champion, and describe her waiting up for him until he staggered home from the Black Bull, to let him in and help him up the stairs. "In that silent home, it was the silent Emily who had ever a cheering word for Branwell; it was Emily who still remembered that he was her brother, without that remembrance freezing her heart to numbness. She still hoped to win him back to love; and the very force and sincerity of his guilty passion (an additional horror and sin in her sisters' eyes) was a claim on Emily, ever sympathetic to violent feeling."[49] The image fits the author of the Gondal poems and *Wuthering Heights,* and it is accepted by Winifred Gérin, the foremost authority on the Brontës, who believes that Emily died of grief for her brother and that Branwell's ruin was a major factor in her loss of imaginative power.[50] Her moral vision was not of the conventional kind, and she and Branwell had identified before as exiles from society. In the face of this, it seems almost unfeeling to point out, as Laura Hinkley does, that there is no evidence for what has virtually become an Emily Brontë legend, or that after one of his drunks, Emily called Branwell "a hopeless being."[51]

However strong Brontë's sympathies were, living with Branwell was both perilous and harrowing. Once, he set his bed on fire and lay in it stupefied. While Charlotte and Anne shrunk helplessly against the wall, Emily went downstairs to the kitchen, where the family kept buckets of water. Returning with one in each hand, she put out the fire, dragged the unconscious Branwell out of the room, and put him in her own bed.[52] After this, Mr. Brontë took in Branwell to sleep with him. Knowing that their father kept loaded pistols in his room, the sisters feared that Branwell would do violence, either against his father or himself, and they lay listening "for the report of a pistol in the dead of the night, till watchful eye and hearkening ear grew heavy and dull with the perpetual strain upon their nerves."[53] Although Branwell's worst period came after the completion of *Wuthering Heights,* the violence of his love and his despair undoubtedly influenced Emily in the creation of Hindley Earnshaw, and it would have been from Branwell, more than anyone else, that Emily derived her image of the male.

Branwell died suddenly, on September 24, 1848, a Sunday. At his funeral service, a week later, Brontë caught a severe cold which developed with deadly speed into inflammation of the lungs and consumption. She never left the house again.

The story of Brontë's death only intensifies the mystery of her life. She would not admit that she was ill, but insisted on rising and dressing as usual, and dragging herself about the house to do her usual tasks. Less than a week before she died, she tried to feed the dogs and almost fell from weakness. Her sisters came forward, begging her to let them help her—she waved them away. She refused to see a doctor or take any medicine, and would not listen to the advice which Charlotte, in desperation, had obtained by letter from a physician. They could all see that Anne, who had always been sickly, was visibly dying as well, whereas Emily had always been the strongest in the family and the last to complain of the bitter winter winds and the parsonage's cold stone floors. Whether she thought that an effort of will would enable her to overcome the infirmities of the flesh, or whether she was hastening to die and fulfilling a death wish that runs through her writing, we will never know—she told no one how or what she felt. On December 19, she dressed and went into the parlor where Anne and Charlotte were seated, and attempted to sew. At noon, she told her sisters that if they would send for a doctor, she would see one now. Two hours later Emily Brontë was dead. She was thirty years and five months old.

Chapter Two
Reconstructing Gondal

We have seen that Emily Brontë spent the greater part of her adult life absorbed in her story about Gondal and its people. The notebook which she called "Gondal Poems," when she began to make fair copies of her work in February 1844, contained only the forty-five Gondal poems which she considered finished, or which she composed after that date. At least 117 of her 195 poems are definitely or very probably Gondal poems, and they exist in several manuscript and printed sources.[1] In addition, Brontë wrote a considerable amount of Gondal prose. In 1845, Anne wrote in her diary paper that "Emily is engaged in writing the Emperor Julius's life. She has read some of it, and I want very much to hear the rest. She is writing some poetry, too. I wonder what it is about. . . . We have not yet finished our Gondal Chronicles that we began three years and a half ago." In her companion note, Brontë says she is "writing a work on the First Wars."[2] Eight years earlier, in 1837, she was at work on the first volume of the life of her heroine, Augusta Almeda. The Gondal venture went on from apprenticeship to maturity, and a story which could engross Brontë for so long ought to throw a special light on the imagination that it shaped. Gondal, after all, was more than just make-believe or a game; it was Brontë's myth.

But the task of reconstructing Gondal is a formidable one, "about as difficult," as Derek Stanford says, "as would be that of reconstructing Shakespeare's plays (supposing them to have perished) from the snatches of song they included. . . ."[3] All of the Gondal prose has disappeared; and the poems, written as lyrical accompaniments to the prose, illuminate only isolated and dispersed portions of the narrative. Thus, all "reconstructions" of Gondal depend largely on conjecture and inference, and though I will speak of Alfred as being Augusta's second husband, there is no direct mention of either of them having ever been married. We have, in fact, less than the skeleton of what was an expansive, dynastic myth; and our task, to use a different, more familiar metaphor, is like that of rebuilding the likeness of some extinct species, with only a piece of leg bone, a foot print, and half of a lower jaw to work with. It is even more difficult for us in that the paleontologist can draw on his knowledge of comparative anatomy as a guide, whereas Gondal was unique.

Even the best authorities disagree about the fundamental pattern of the story. The two principal figures in the Gondal poems, for instance, are Julius Brenzaida of Angora and Augusta G. Almeda (or A. G. A.)—an emperor and an empress of Gondal and Gaaldine. Laura Hinkley argues that Augusta was the daughter of Julius and Geraldine Sidonia. After her mother was drowned bringing her to Gondal, Augusta is brought up in the mountains of Angora, while her father rules in court with his second wife, Rosina of Alcona.[4] According to Fannie Ratchford, however, Augusta, Rosina, and Geraldine are the same woman, who becomes Julius's wife.[5] For W. D. Paden, the three women are separate characters, and there is no relation or involvement between Augusta and Julius.[6] I find Paden's version of the story to be the most convincing of any advanced so far, but such fundamental differences are a warning of the uncertain ground any investigation of Gondal must rest on.

Difficulties arise not only from the loss of the Gondal prose, but from the way Brontë condensed and obscured the information in her poems. Many poems have no names attached to them to indicate their speakers; others are prefaced with initials, which may refer to the speaker of the poem or the person the speaker addresses. A set of initials, such as A. S., may belong to more than one character—in this case a father and daughter. A character may have more than one name or title and be named differently in different poems: Julius Brenzaida, because of his territories in Gondal and Gaaldine, is "Julius Angora" and "Almedore." There are initials for which no name exists in the poems, and we cannot always distinguish a speaker's sex. And while it is usually clear which poems belong to the Gondal story and which are Brontë's personal, non-Gondal lyrics, the distinction is not always or uniformly apparent. For several poems it is impossible to be sure.

Moreover, the order in which Brontë wrote her poems does not correspond to the chronology of events in the Gondal narrative. On May 20, 1838, Brontë wrote of Augusta mourning over the dying Alfred; two years later, she wrote of their first falling in love. A poem written April 20, 1839, tells us that Julius has been murdered; in 1843, Brontë described one of Julius's battles in Gaaldine; and in a poem dated November 11, 1844, Julius has not yet gone to Gaaldine. Brontë's poetic imagination, then, moved backwards and forwards over the Gondal narrative; and her poems, in their order of composition, read like a stream-of-consciousness novel, using flashback and multiple points of view.

It will be more helpful, I think, to state what we can be reasonably sure of, before beginning the reconstruction of the story.

Gondal was a large island in the North Pacific, with a climate and terrain like that of Brontë's Yorkshire: cold winters, mountains, and moor country. It was divided into several kingdoms, principally Exina in the south and Angora in the north; the capital city of the whole was Regina. Gaaldine was a large island in the South Pacific, which was discovered and explored by Gondal adventurers. It was divided into a large province (Zedora) and five kingdoms: Alexandia, Almedore, Elseraden, Ula, and Zalona or Zelona.[7] Although it has winters too, Gaaldine seems to have been more tropical than Gondal.

Fannie Ratchford identifies the three main periods of the Gondal saga as consisting of (1) the discovery and conquest of Gaaldine, to which none of the poems refer; (2) the First Wars, in Gondal and Gaaldine, to which the great majority of the poems belong; (3) the republican revolution and civil war, which is dealt with in about half a dozen poems.[8] Gondal time is earlier than Haworth time, and from Gondal dates which Brontë used in five of her poems to distinguish the time at which Gondal events were meant to occur from the time at which she was writing about them, we can conclude that Gaaldine was discovered and settled by 1825. The period of the First Wars, when Julius rose to power and became emperor, was 1825–1830. After his death, Augusta ruled for a decade or more, so that the time of the civil wars, following her death, is virtually approximate to Haworth time (the middle 1840's). Admittedly, there is no definitive proof that Augusta ruled after Julius, but all of the evidence points to that conclusion, even if Brontë did not intend (which is hardly possible) "Julius" and "Augusta" to recall their Roman namesakes.

The following is a partial list of the dramatis personae in Brontë's Gondal poems.[9]

Julius Brenzaida	King of Angora in Gondal and of Almedore in Gaaldine; Emperor of Gondal and Gaaldine. He is associated with Geraldine S., who bears him a child, and Rosina Alcona. Assassinated.
Alexander of Elbë (A. E.)	Augusta Almeda's first husband (or lover). Killed in a battle by Lake Elnor in Gondal.
Alfred S. (A. S.)	Lord of Aspin Hall, and the second husband (or lover) of Augusta Almeda. A member of the Exina family and the brother of Gerald Exina and Geraldine S. Dies in exile.
Gerald of Exina (G. S.)	King of Gondal. After Julius defeats his forces in war, the two are crowned joint emperors. Julius has Gerald imprisoned. Dies in prison.
Fernando De Samara	One of Augusta's cast-off lovers. Commits suicide.
Amedeus	Another of Augusta's cast-off lovers; he had been the early lover of Angelica. Killed in an act of violence, possibly against Julius.
Douglas	An outlaw. He murders Augusta, and is almost certainly involved in the assassination of Julius.
The Glenedens	A large family allied to the Exinas in the conspiracy against Julius.
H. A.	H. Angora? Probably the son of Julius and Geraldine; as a young man he resembles Alfred.
Augusta G. Almeda (A. G. A.)	Empress and Queen of Gondal and Gaaldine, and the central figure of the Gondal saga. Assassinated.
Rosina Alcona	Julius's first lover and probably his second wife. Though politically ambitious, she is faithful to Julius.
Geraldine S. (G.S.)	Julius's first wife and the sister of Gerald and Alfred. After the birth of her child, she disappears from the story.

Angelica
(A. S.)

She once loved Augusta, but became her sworn enemy, and plots her assassination. Probably—but not certainly—the daughter of Alfred and an unknown first wife.

Alexandria
(A. A., A. A. A.,
A. S.)

A young woman who resembles Augusta and who is probably the daughter of Augusta and Alfred. She survives after Augusta abandons her in a snow storm.

Blanche

Augusta's lady in waiting. She rescues the infant Alexandria and takes her to Gaaldine.

The Gondal Saga

In 1825, Gondal time, Julius Brenzaida, a young man from a noble family, has been imprisoned for moral dereliction, and he is rebuked by an elderly judge for putting pleasure before duty. Julius, in turn, blames his absent paramour, Rosina Alcona. Had it not been for her and her influence on him, he would now be sailing with his companions to Gaaldine.[10] We learn that Rosina is an ambitious woman capable of arousing strong passions in men without becoming enslaved to them herself. She could be among those who are sailing to Gaaldine, because after his release from prison Julius becomes involved with and marries another woman, Geraldine S.—probably a member of the Exina family and sister of Gerald, the Gondal monarch, and Alfred S. She insists that she accompany Julius to Gaaldine, and receives an angry rebuke from him, which Brontë entitled "Song by J. Brenzaida to G. S.":

> I knew not 'twas so dire a crime
> To say the word, Adieu;
> But this shall be the only time
> My slighted heart shall sue.
> (#81, p. 83)

If she cannot remain loyal to him in his absence, then he can as easily forget her. There are other women whose love he has already proved—presumably Rosina's. We learn little more about Geraldine except that she does go to Gaaldine, either with Julius or after him, and she gives birth there to Julius's child (sex undisclosed) in a cave, away from her friends, with only one companion to care for her (#150, pp. 168–69). Geraldine is a tender, clinging woman who has been deserted by Julius.

Julius is in the Gaaldine phase of the First Wars, and wages a vicious and victorious battle against the followers and territories of the Exina family. After a brutal and starkly described siege, he captures the capital city of the Gaaldine kingdom of Zalona, reducing its inhabitants almost to cannibalism (#156, pp. 181–84). Sometime later, he crosses the sea for an invasion of Gondal, and forces Gerald Exina to agree to a joint rulership. The two are crowned in a vast cathedral, in the presence of thousands, but Julius is already plotting the treachery by which he will become the sole monarch:

> All mute as death regard the shrine
> That gleams in lustre so divine,
> Where Gondal's monarchs, bending low
> After the hush of silent prayer,
> Take, in heaven's sight, their awful vow,
> And never dying union swear.
> King Julius lifts his impious eye
> From the dark marble to the sky;
> Blasts with that Oath his perjured soul,
> And changeless is his cheek the while,
> Though burning thoughts, that spurn control,
> Kindle a short and bitter smile,
> As face to face the kinsmen stand,
> His false hand clasped in Gerald's hand.
> (#56, pp. 67–68)

That Julius and Gerald are kinsmen strengthens the probability that Geraldine is Gerald's sister, and that Julius has married into the royal family he wages war against. It is not long before Julius has Gerald thrown into prison, where he languishes and dies. This treachery against her brother would complete the alienation between Geraldine and Julius. And with her death (or disappearance) he is free to marry Rosina.

Julius's triumph is shortlived. His treatment of Gerald and his tyrannical rule have created powerful enemies, including the Gleneden family, who are allied to or part of the Exina line. One of them—Arthur Gleneden—has been put in prison, and while there he dreams of stabbing Julius to death and restoring Gondal's liberty (#63, pp. 72–74). The Glenedens and a traitor named Douglas speak of keeping a secret and holy vow. Alfred S., Gerald's brother, is already living in exile, but his daughter, Angelica, remains in Gondal, and Fannie Ratchford believes that the actual assassin of Julius is Angelica's lover, Amedeus.[11] But of him we learn very little. It is most likely that, like the Roman emperor, King Julius is slain by a well-organized faction which, in addition to personal grievances, feared his unchecked ambitions. Brontë tells of Julius's death in a simple and powerful ballad:

> King Julius left the south country
> His banners all bravely flying;
> His followers went out with Jubilee
> But they shall return with sighing.
>
> Loud arose the triumphal hymn
> The drums were loudly rolling,
> Yet you might have heard in distance dim
> How a passing bell was tolling.
>
> The sword so bright from battles won
> With unseen rust is fretting,
> The evening comes before the noon,
> The scarce risen sun is setting.
>
> While princes hang upon his breath
> And nations round are fearing,
> Close by his side a daggered death
> With sheathless point stands sneering.
>
> That death he took a certain aim,
> For Death is stony-hearted
> And in the zenith of his fame
> Both power and life departed.
>   (#98, p. 104)

One of the assassins was killed on the spot. Douglas escapes after a long and thrilling chase. As we shall see, it is an outlaw of the same name who assassinates Augusta Almeda.

Because of a long illness, Rosina was unable to accompany Julius to his palace in Angora, which she thought would be the scene of his greatest triumph. Her ambitions are shattered when she learns of his death from an eye witness (#151, pp. 170–72). Augusta's succession to the throne moves Rosina out of the center of power and influence, yet she remains loyal to Julius, and her love for him is as strong as ever fifteen years after his death. Her lament, "R. Alcona to J. Brenzaida," is one of Brontë's most impassioned poems:

> Cold in the earth, and the deep snow piled above thee!
> Far, far removed, cold in the dreary grave!
> Have I forgot, my Only Love, to love thee,
> Severed at last by Time's all-wearing wave?
>
> Now, when alone, do my thoughts no longer hover
> Over the mountains on Angora's shore;
> Resting their wings where heath and fern-leaves cover
> That noble heart for ever, ever more?
>   (#182, pp. 222–23)

But though she loves him she will not bury her life in the past, and she cannot loosen the hold on her of her renewed ambitions:

> Sweet Love of youth, forgive if I forget thee
> While the World's tide is bearing me along:
> Sterner desires and darker hopes beset me,
> Hopes which obscure but cannot do thee wrong.

Realism and passion combine to make a complex, honest portrait.

We now turn to Augusta G. Almeda, who figures in more Gondal poems than any other character, and whose career has important parallels with that of Julius. She too is imprisoned before her rise to power; she has several love affairs and marriages; and she becomes a domineering ruler who meets a violent end.

At an early age, and before the opening of the story as we have it, Augusta marries Alexander Elbë. For reasons that are not given, the two are parted—probably Alexander goes to Gaaldine and is delayed or occupied there. In his absence, either because she believes him dead or because of her unquenchable passions, Augusta falls in love with another man, Alfred S., and marries him. We know a good deal more about Alfred than about Alexander. Alfred is a fair-complexioned, pious man and the master of Aspin Hall, where he lives with his daughter, who becomes Augusta's stepchild. There is no mention of his first wife: we must assume she has died. According to Paden, Alfred is the brother of Geraldine and Gerald, the head of the Exina line.[12] When questioned by an unnamed speaker about her two lovers, Augusta protests her faithfulness to both, but compares Alexander to the moon and Alfred to the sun. A small love sufficed, she says, until a greater love shone upon her, and "could the day seem dark to me / Because the night was fair?" (#110, p. 118). But then Alexander returns to Gondal, and there is a battle by the shores of Lake Elnor in midsummer, in which someone—presumably Alfred—defeats and kills Alexander. It is with this event, Augusta's memory of holding the dying Alexander in her arms, that Brontë began her Gondal notebook.[13]

The dying Alexander, realizing that he will never return to his home, accuses Augusta of shallowness:

> "Augusta—you will soon return
> Back to that land in health and bloom
> And then the heath alone will mourn
> Above my unremembered tomb,
> For you'll forget the lonely grave
> And mouldering corpse by Elnor's wave."
>
> (#9, p. 35)

But he could not be more wrong. His words and tragic death haunt Augusta's imagination, which compulsively recreates the scene at Lake Elnor, or envisions the gaunt wreck of Elbë Hall, where they had lived. At the same time, Augusta is devoted and attached to Alfred, who must leave her for permanent exile in England. It is apparent that Alfred either did not know of Augusta and Alexander, or was assured by Augusta of Alexander's death—though the former seems more likely to me. In either case, the consequences of Augusta's sin fall on Alfred, who has been led into murder. At their parting, Augusta admits her guilt and Alfred's innocence:

> I know that I have done thee wrong—
> Have wronged both thee and Heaven—

And I may mourn my lifetime long
Yet may not be forgiven.

Repentant tears will vainly fall
To cancel deeds untrue;
But for no grief can I recall
The dreary word—Adieu.

Yet thou a future peace shalt win
Because thy soul is clear;
And I who had the heart to sin
Will find a heart to bear.

Till far beyond earth's frenzied strife
That makes destruction joy,
Thy perished faith shall spring to life
And my remorse shall die.
                    (#169, pp. 197–98)

She obviously regrets the necessity of his leaving, and sometime later
Augusta journeys to England. She is with Alfred, as she was with
Alexander, when he dies:

The grave must close those limbs around,
And hush, for ever hush the tone
I loved above all earthly sound.
                    (#61, p. 71)

Augusta's hopes that their penance will restore Alfred's faith and
expiate her crime are not fulfilled. In a poem entitled "Written in
Aspin Castle" (#154, pp. 175–79), we learn that Alfred's ghost haunts
his old home, and that his unforgiven spirit "Wanders unsheltered,
shut from heaven— / An outcast for eternity." And for Augusta, who
stole Alfred's affections away from his daughter, the speaker has nothing but scorn:

There is no worm, however mean,
That. living, is not nobler now
Than she, Lord Alfred's idol queen,
So loved, so worshipped, long ago.

Augusta's morals degenerate after Alfred's exile. She attracts lovers, grows tired of them, and casts them off. One, Fernando De Samara, she has imprisoned. Later, when he commits suicide, he upbraids her bitterly for her treachery. If he could make her feel one-tenth of the pain that tortures him, he says, he would feel revenged (#85, pp. 85–87). Back in her palace, Augusta has forgotten him, and as she touches the guitar Fernando used to play, she wonders that her heart should be so dry of feeling for him who played it (#76, p. 80). In "The Death of A. G. A." (#143, pp. 150–61), Angelica curses Augusta for first enticing Amedeus away from her and then, when tired of him, sending the two into exile.

Augusta's reign is longer than Julius's, and apparently the country is at peace while she rules. But Angelica remains her bitter enemy, wandering the empty moor country with the outlaw Douglas. One day Augusta, with just two companions, goes to Elmor (or Elnor) hill, near the spot where Alexander died, and Angelica sees her chance. She promises to become Douglas's lover if he will help her kill the three of them. Armed with daggers, they surprise and easily murder the young man and woman who had accompanied the Queen, but when Douglas attacks Augusta, she puts up a savage fight:

> She turns—she meets the Murderer's gaze;
> Her own is scorched with a sudden blaze—
> The blood streams down her brow;
> The blood streams through her coal-black hair—
> She strikes it off with little care;
> She scarcely feels it flow;
> For she has marked and known him too
> And his own heart's ensanguined dew
> Must slake her vengeance now.
> (#143, p. 158)

Angelica holds back from the fight and waits only to see that Augusta is dying before she abandons the wounded Douglas, who leaves a trail of blood for Augusta's men to follow when they arrive at the scene.

Their leader is Lord Eldred, who has known Augusta all of her life and been her counselor. He reviews the rise and fall of one who was adored as an idol, and who did not always use her power wisely or humanely:

> For what thou wert I would not grieve,
> But much for what thou wert to be—
> That life so stormy and so brief,
> That death has wronged us more than thee.
> Thy passionate youth was nearly past,
> The opening sea seemed smooth at last;
>   (#143, p. 161)

—but fate decreed that she would not reach life's calmer waters. "The Death of A. G. A." is Brontë's longest poem; and according to the dates which she affixed to it (January 1841–May 1844), she worked on it for three and a half years. It brings to an end the first generation of Gondalans—Julius, Gerald, Alfred, Alexander, Geraldine, Augusta: all but Rosina are dead. The country is now threatened with civil war.

Brontë meant to continue the story into a second generation, but of this only a few fragments and hints remain. Geraldine, we saw, gave birth to Julius's child in a cave in Gaaldine—an infant with dark eyes like its father's. We may assume, although we do not know, that this is a boy and that he survives. Alfred has a fair-haired daughter who grew up in Aspin Hall with Augusta, and who would have good reason to feel betrayed by Augusta because of the banishment of her father. We can identify her with the "fair" Angelica of "The Death of A. G. A.," although now her "locks" are "dark and long," and she is bitter about the treatment of Amedeus. In one of the later poems, entitled "Castle Wood," the speaker is identified as A. S., but is almost certainly not Alfred. The voice is disillusioned and hard, and speaks of its heart as being "dead since infancy," whereas Alfred, at least until his exile, is devout and trusting. It is either Angelica S. who would speak words like,

> No star will light my coming night;
> No moon of hope for me will shine;
> I mourn not heaven would blast my sight,
> And I never longed for ways divine.
>   (#167, p. 195)

—or else someone very like her. It is very probable that Angelica has a half sister, Alexandria, the child of Augusta and Alfred. Because

Augusta was still married to Alexander when she married Alfred, her child by the latter would be illegitimate, and thus block or threaten her succession to the throne. With one husband dead and the other in exile, Augusta abandons the child in a snowstorm (#108, pp. 114–15); shortly afterwards, Augusta is put in prison.

But there are reasons for thinking the child does not die. Augusta's companion, Blanche, rescued the child and took her to Gaaldine (#62, pp. 71–72), where she grew up in one of the palaces, friendless, before returning to Gondal. Alexandria's initials are given as A. A.— Alexandria Almeda, after her mother—though as Alfred's child she could also be designated as A. S.[14] Brontë was undecided about the color of Alexandria's hair.[15] Alexandria is a melancholy child, gifted musically, and she and Augusta live in the same palace in Gondal, but do not recognize each other. Augusta believes that Alexandria died in the snow.

Years after the courtship of Augusta and Alfred, someone who knows their story is struck by the resemblance to them in another youthful pair, only now the boy is dark instead of fair, and the girl is fair instead of dark:

> In the same place, when Nature wore
> The same celestial glow,
> I'm sure I've seen those forms before
> But many springs ago;
>
> And only *he* had locks of light,
> And *she* had raven hair;
> While now, his curls are dark as night,
> And hers as morning fair.
> (#153, pp. 173–74)

The title of the poem is "H. A. and A. S." As the speaker goes on to describe the earlier pair, they are unquestionably Augusta and Alfred; the most likely conjecture is that H. A. is H. Angora—the son of Geraldine and Julius Angora and thus Alfred's nephew—while A. S. is Alexandria. The two are, then, first cousins, and as a number of commentators have pointed out, they foreshadow Hareton Earnshaw and Cathy Linton, who bear the same relationship to each other and have the same appearance. With royal blood from both parents, H. A. and A. S. would become the next heirs to the throne. But at that point, the Gondal dynasty ceases as mysteriously as it began.

The Gondal Imagination

Although the Gondal story was of major importance to Brontë herself, even more so than her published work, its importance for us, as readers of her poems and *Wuthering Heights,* is much more difficult to determine or to agree on. Fannie Ratchford arranges the poems to make a novel in verse about the life of Augusta Almeda; and she argues that "all of Emily's verse, as we have it, falls within the Gondal context."[16] Mary Visick, tracing the order in which Brontë placed her poems in the Gondal notebook, finds a number of parallels to the story, characters, and emotions of *Wuthering Heights.*[17] At the other extreme, Derek Stanford contends that the Gondal whole—as distinguished from individual poems—is marred by melodrama and bad writing, and that attempts to reconstruct the Gondal story obstruct our criticism of Emily Brontë's art.[18] Hence, we have those who see Gondal permeating virtually everything Brontë wrote and inseparable from it, and those who want to dismiss it altogether. And both, as a matter of fact, make a valid if limited case. We can read *Wuthering Heights,* as most of its readers do, without venturing into Gondal at all. At the same time, the Gondal legend nourished and shaped the imagination that produced *Wuthering Heights,* and that was not limited to Gondal material. Possibly, Emily Brontë would have outgrown the Gondal story had she lived longer, but without the years she spent creating the story, developing her Gondal imagination, the mature imagination she did attain would have been a considerably different mode of vision.

The Gondal imagination was one which concerned itself with the fate of dynasties and kingdoms, with large scale traumatic events affecting the whole state: conquests, wars, assassinations. There are virtually no domestic scenes in the Gondal poems, and no concern with the minutiae of daily life. We learn nothing about Gondalan dress or social manners. We do not know what the Gondals ate or what they read, whether they went to the theater, or whether there were theaters or other places of amusement for them to attend. Like the people in *Wuthering Heights,* Gondalans live stark, elemental lives; they love and hate violently and in extremes; and most often they are alone—confronting the vast, unpeopled landscapes of nature, or the isolated universe of their inner passions. The most vividly realized moments of time in the story seem to transcend time and become eternal or omnipresent, as the death of Alexander repeats itself unmercifully in Augusta's mind to become one of its permanent fixtures; or, as Brontë breaks up the Gondal chronology in the sequence of her composition, Julius is at once the slain ruler and the object of an extended plot to assassinate him.

Brontë's characters are both heroic, larger than life, and flawed or limited, and their image for us shifts as we see them from their own point of view and from that of their victims and enemies. The Augusta who mourns over Alfred and Alexander speaks as a conscience-stricken, almost tender woman; to Fernando and Angelica, she is a cold-blooded tyrant. We see Julius in the objective, impersonal terms of the ballad, "King Julius left the south country," and in the intensely personal terms of the Glenedens' hate and Rosina's love. His and Augusta's careers, and the Gondal story as we have it, are constructed out of different, intersecting moral and emotional attitudes to the same person or event. In a similar manner, the three principal women—Augusta, Rosina, and Geraldine—divide the image of a woman in love into three different subimages or alternative roles. Augusta is aggressive and pleasure-seeking, and she dominates or destroys her lovers. The more passive Geraldine is dominated by Julius, and we see her only in the traditional roles of wife and mother. Although Rosina remains faithful to one man, she puts love and the lover's role second to her political ambitions. Indeed, Brontë's women are as free in their thought and action as her men are, and they strive as resolutely for the same or similar ends. Brontë herself, in the meantime, offers no definitive, authorial opinion or verdict on any of her characters. We must judge the Gondals entirely from within their own frame of reference.

For most of us, the Gondal imagination is marked by its obscurity—its use of private symbols and cryptic allusions which show only the tip of the iceberg, as in this example, headed A. G. A. and dated March 27, 1839:

> What winter floods, what showers of spring
> Have drenched the grass by night and day;

> And yet, beneath, that spectre ring,
> Unmoved and undiscovered lay
>
> A mute remembrancer of crime,
> Long lost, concealed, forgot for years,
> It comes at last to cancel time,
> And waken unavailing tears.
>   (#96, pp. 101–102)

Both Paden, who omits the comma after "ring," and Ratchford conclude that a long-lost ring has been returned to Augusta, which is of course a possible reading, and that the ring reminds her of a crime.[19] But it is also possible that "spectre ring" refers to the plot of grass Augusta has returned to, and that beneath it lies the "mute remembrancer of crime"—the bones of the infant she abandoned in the snowstorm, or of one of her old lovers. We simply do not know. The poem's meaning is condensed to, or contained in, an image, and is at once elusive and compact.

Brontë's poetry is most elusive when it is most connected to her private world, but even then its meaning need not be totally obscure. "What winter floods" also connects to other poems in the Gondal story, in which Augusta feels guilt, and to poems in which a particular spot or place obsesses her. The crime remains conjectural; the figure haunted by a crime and drawn to its scene stands out sharply. In another poem, Augusta asks, "Why do I hate that lone green dell" (#60, pp. 69–70); and when she abandons her child, it is in a dell (#108, p. 114). Perhaps the three places are the same; but what matters more is the framework and intensity of emotion which Emily Brontë is able to convey in her lean, demanding verse. The characters that the emotions attach to become, in the best poems, unforgettable figures, at once individualized and symbolic. Brontë knew them all so intimately she could refer to them at times by their initials only, and thus preserve their anonymity while she brought out and expressed their personalities. And no doubt the device made it easier for her to keep her story a secret, even as she peopled it with representatives of mankind.

Chapter Three

Poetry

Unlike *Wuthering Heights,* which was controversial in its own time and is widely read today, Emily Brontë's poetry has remained relatively unknown, except to specialists. Critics have tended to agree with what Charlotte Brontë said of her sister's poems, when she read Emily's manuscript book in 1845: ". . . something more than surprise seized me,—a deep conviction that these were not common effusions, nor at all like the poetry women generally write. I thought them condensed and terse, vigorous and genuine."[1] But criticism of Brontë's poetry has never been a flourishing industry, and as a poet, Emily Brontë has not been accorded the major recognition which the twentieth century has given to other nineteenth-century unknowns, such as Emily Dickinson and Gerard Manley Hopkins. Even now, her poems are studied mostly as foreshadowings of *Wuthering Heights,* as autobiography, or as clues to the nebulous Gondal puzzle.[2] Numerous editions of *Wuthering Heights* continue to appear; Brontë's poems, on the other hand, are either omitted from anthologies of Victorian poetry or represented by a small handful that gives no indication of her range and achievement. Hatfield's excellent edition is not readily accessible to the student or the general reader, who often overlooks the fact, or is simply unaware of it, that the famous author of *Wuthering Heights* also wrote almost two hundred poems. An important and distinctive voice in English poetry has still to receive the notice it deserves.

Emily Brontë wrote all of her known poetry between 1836 and 1846, a decade which saw the emergence of such major poets as Tennyson and Browning, who would reshape the Romantic tradition which they inherited. Brontë is at once a contributor and an outsider to this period of transition. She taught herself to extend the Romantic lyric outward from personal feeling to objective characterization, and at the same time as Browning she was experimenting with the form of the dramatic monologue. Like all the major Romantic and Victorian poets, Brontë was deeply concerned with the creative imagination as the source of the higher truth of poetry; and she wrote some of her best poems to question and affirm the nature and validity of her imaginative vision. But Brontë was a self-taught, highly individual poet who lived and wrote in isolation. Unlike her contemporaries, she did not address her poetry to the major issues of her times—the conflicts that were coming to a head because of the industrial revolution or the growing evidence for the theory of evolution. Although a visionary, she did not think of herself as a prophet; and although she was concerned with the meaning of life and death, she did not write, as Tennyson and Arnold did, a poetry of ideas, or of moral and social commentary. Undoubtedly, she was influenced by her readings in Byron and Scott, and by the evangelical Christianity of her father and her aunt, but her poetry is not a derivative one, and it does not follow literary fashions or refer back to a collective system of belief.

To Emily Dickinson, she was "gigantic Emily Brontë."[3] As we shall see, her themes have cosmic implications and deal with man's relationships to an absolute power. Her stylistic devices, which we will consider first, anticipate the modern age of relativity. Brontë's poetry leans much more to the imagistic than the discursive, to the poem as a slice of life rather than an application of ideas to life. Her poems range from simple songs to stark and often violent narratives to psychological monologues; and Brontë was not afraid to undercut in one poem a position or attitude she had developed in another. Although individually, her poems are simple and direct, their combined vision of life is complex. Subjectivity fades into objectivity in her poetry, without a clear line of demarcation between their two realms of truth. Her ability to combine lyrical expressiveness with dramatic portrait enabled her to express with equal intensity and detachment her personal emotions and those of an imagined character—so successful is she, in fact, that critics disagree sharply over which voice in the poems is Brontë's as opposed to the impersonative voice of a Gondalan. Even when we can tell Brontë's voice, it cannot be said to have a different weight or authority than the other voices. Her achievement was great. She created a gallery of characters, including the "I" that represents herself, so that she could explore the possibilities of human experience from as many vantage points as possible, without committing herself entirely to one.

Identifying Emily Brontë's Speakers

Brontë's ability to combine lyric expressiveness and dramatic portraiture of character appears in an early poem, written May 17, 1837, when Brontë was eighteen, the age of the speaker in the poem. The speaker's disenchantment with life, however, is an attitude that occurs frequently among the Gondalans, yet there is no direct Gondal reference. We cannot even be sure of the speaker's sex. The poem illustrates the problem that appears often in Brontë's work of distinguishing self-portrait from dramatic character, Brontë's own voice from an assumed voice, and the real world of Haworth from the Gondal fantasy.

I am the only being whose doom
No tongue would ask, no eye would mourn;
I never caused a thought of gloom,
A smile of joy, since I was born.

In secret pleasure, secret tears,
This changeful life has slipped away,
As friendless after eighteen years,
As lone as on my natal day.

There have been times I cannot hide,
There have been times when this was drear,
When my sad soul forgot its pride
And longed for one to love me here.

But those were in the early glow
Of feelings since subdued by care;
And they have died so long ago,
I hardly now believe they were.

First melted off the hope of youth,
Then fancy's rainbow fast withdrew;
And then experience told me truth
In mortal bosoms never grew.

'Twas grief enough to think mankind
All hollow, servile, insincere;

> But worse to trust to my own mind
> And find the same corruption there.[4]
>   (#11, p. 36)

There is no evidence that at eighteen Brontë felt this bitterly or strongly about mankind and her own condition, and it would be wrong to read the poem as an autobiography. At the same time it presents a point of view and a darkness with the intimacy of firsthand experience. Charles Morgan is probably right to say that the Gondal poems liberated Brontë's personal feelings, but "I am the only being whose doom" is more than a "cloak for personal feeling."[5] It suggests instead that Brontë felt as intensely for what she experienced in imagination as for what she experienced in her more mundane life.

To compound the problem, we find the attitude of the doomed youth repeated in two poems written in the spring of 1839. The first is "The soft unclouded blue of air," in which another unidentified speaker describes an "iron man." Seen from the outside, the iron man bears a strong resemblance to the youth we have seen from the inside, although his childhood seems to have been brighter. Now, however, his heart is hardened, and nature has no influence on him:

> One glance revealed how little care
> He felt for all the beauty there.
>
> Oh, crime can make the heart grow old
> Sooner than years of wearing woe;
> Can turn the warmest bosom cold
> As winter wind or polar snow.
>   (#99, p. 106)

Although there are strong Gondal overtones to the poem, there is again no direct reference to anything Gondalan. All we can be certain of, in the two poems under discussion, is the dual presentation from the inside and from the outside of, if not the same individual, at least the same type of person. That he is now an iron *man,* of course, indicates that the portrait is more definitly dramatic and objective.

But a month later, Brontë wrote "May flowers are opening," a poem which she signed with her own name, and in which she expressed virtually the same hardened attitude as the iron man's. We go back inside the disillusioned mind of one who is impervious or indifferent to nature:

> The sun is gladly shining,
> The stream sings merrily,
> And I only am pining
> And all is dark to me.
>
> O cold, cold is my heart!
> It will not, cannot rise;
> It feels no sympathy
> With those refulgent skies.
>
> Dead, dead is my joy,
> I long to be at rest;
> I wish the damp earth covered
> This desolate breast.
>   (#101, p. 108)

The doomed youth spoke of the corruption that had overtaken his mind; Brontë speaks of her cold heart and her dark vision. Between them is the iron man whose bosom is as "cold" as the polar snow. One poem is clearly self-expressive; one is almost certainly objective and impersonal; and one, "I am the only being whose doom," is ambiguously positioned between the two.

The three poems do not portray the same individual, and even the Emily Brontë whose joy is dead need not be identified with the doomed youth. Rather they evoke the same symbol. The doomed youth, the iron man, and Brontë in "May flowers are opening" have lost the capacity to feel positive emotion. They have become hollow men, who can respond only negatively to life and to themselves. They speak or are described to us, appropriately enough, in a plain, factual language, as if to stress this inability to overcome their loss of feeling. The procedure by which Brontë depicts the hollow man first in his own voice, as the doomed youth, and then from the outside, as the iron man, and finally in her own voice, does make it difficult sometimes to identify her personae or to know which speak in her voice and which do not. But the device also taught her the resources of point of view, and gave her a technique which she further developed in the Gondal poems. There we find interior and exterior revelations of character taking place among the characters themselves, as the self-portrait of one Gondalan merges with or clashes against his image in the minds of others.

Characterization from Divergent Points of View

Emily Brontë understood that perception changes with the perceiver, and in her Gondal narrative she used different poems to delineate characters from both their own point of view and from that of others. One view is not necessarily more valid or objective than another, and the composite picture of a character joins self-portrait with the often different impressions of the character upon others. Julius Angora is a tyrant to those who opposed him in war; he is the object of Rosina's only and enduring love; and he thinks of himself as a strong and capable leader. With such conflicting evidence, and with no assurance that all of the evidence has been found, Brontë does not pass moral judgment on her characters. Instead, the "I" that speaks for itself in one poem shrinks or expands, is approved or condemned, as it is spoken of by the "I" of other poems.

Brontë uses these contrasting perceptions most thoroughly in her characterization of her heroine, Augusta Almeda. When Augusta portrays herself, we see and hear a woman dominated and victimized by her strong loves. She is passionate, almost too full of feeling. She remains loyal to Alexander, and her heart would glow if she could hear the sound of his voice again (#16, p. 44). But he is dead, and the memory of his death torments her. In "O Day! He cannot die," she relives the awful moment when she pleaded with him to resist death:

> "It is not Death, but pain
> That struggles in thy breast;
> Nay, rally, Elbë, rouse again,
> I cannot let thee rest!"
> (#180, p. 218)

Her love for Alfred, as we have seen, is just as strong. He is her golden June, and their love for each other is the shrine where she will offer worship:

> I have one rite: a gentle kiss;
> One penance: tender tears.
>
> O could it thus forever be
> That I might so adore;
> I'd ask for all eternity
> To make a paradise for me,
> My love—and nothing more!
>   (#137, p. 144)

There is no suggestion that her attachment to either is not genuine or that it is anything less than a deep emotional involvement. She acknowledges her part in the tragedy that killed one of her lovers and banished the other, and she does not treat her guilt lightly. If indeed it is Augusta who abandons the child in "Farewell to Alexandria," she feels intense anguish and pain at having to do it. From her own perspective, she is a tragic figure, haunted by remorse and loss of innocence, burdened with a secret sorrow or guilt:

> Why do I hate that lone green dell?
> Buried in moors and mountains wild,
> That is a spot I had loved too well
> Had I but seen it when a child.
>
> There are bones whitening there in the summer's heat,
> But it is not for that, and none can tell;
> None but one can the secret repeat
> Why I hate that lone green dell.
>   (#60, p. 69)

The difference between the passionate, tragedy-scarred image of Augusta's self-portrait and her image in the minds of others is startling. The speaker of "Written in Aspin Castle" denounces her as vainglorious and proud (#154, p. 178). Lord Eldred looks upon her dead body as a "wreck of desolate despair" (#143, p. 160). Later, he describes her life as a heedless pursuit of pleasure leading to the smash-up of her soul:

> Why did the pilot, too confiding,
> Dream o'er that Ocean's foam,

> And trust in Pleasure's careless guiding
> To bring his vessel home?
>   (#171, p. 202)

Whereas we see, from inside Augusta, a strong sense of loyalty and
moral consciousness, Lord Eldred sees a weak or corrupted reason
abandoning its charge. Angelica sees Augusta as a witch-woman, a
demon of betrayal and treachery:

> "But cursed be the very earth
> That gave that fiend her fatal birth!
> With her own hand she bent the bow
> That laid my best affections low,
> Then mocked my grief and scorned my prayers
> And drowned my bloom of youth in tears.
> Warnings, reproaches, both were vain—
> What recked she of another's pain?"
>   (#143, p. 153)

But Lord Leslie, one of Augusta's two companions slain by Angelica
and Douglas, in "The Death of A. G. A.," calls for God's blessing on
the queen: "God, guard her life . . . / God, bless her arm with victory /
Or bless not me with heaven" (#143, p. 156). And against Douglas,
Augusta fights with courage and clear-headedness.

Perhaps the bitterest portrait of Augusta is drawn by Fernando De
Samara in two long monologues, the first written at the time of his
suicide on a bleak moor, the second when he is still in prison. In the
latter, Fernando calls Augusta a "false friend and guide," and he accuses
her of delighting in and satiating her cruel heart with his torment:

> Then come again—thou wilt not shrink;
> I know thy soul is free from fear—
> The last full cup of triumph drink,
> Before the blank of death be there.
>
> Thy raving, dying victim see,
> Lost, cursed, degraded, all for thee!
> Gaze on the wretch, recall to mind
> His golden days left long behind.
>   (#133, p. 139)

As Fernando is dying, his mind is so filled with memories of Augusta and the love for her that he cannot control, he imagines her to be possessed of an equally strong hate for him (#85, pp. 85–87). It never occurs to Fernando, obsessed as he is with his own sufferings and injustices, that the "Tyrant" who "rules [him] still" may have utterly forgotten him.

The situation allows Brontë to draw another powerful contrast between the Fernando who appears in the self-portrait of his monologues and the Fernando who appears in Augusta's mind. Fernando's feelings are frenzied and passionate, and before he stabs himself he looks at a picture of Augusta which he carries with him:

> Do I not see thee now? Thy black resplendent hair;
> Thy glory-beaming brow, and smile, how heavenly fair!
> Thine eyes are turned away—those eyes I would not see;
> Their dark, their deadly ray, would more than madden me.
>
> There, go, Deceiver, go! My hand is streaming wet;
> My heart's blood flows to buy the blessing—To forget!
>
> (#85, p. 86)

While in prison, Fernando asks the spirit of memory to recall to Augusta the time when they were lovers and she asked him to play his guitar to her by the shores of Lake Elderno (#133, pp. 139–40). Augusta, however, has virtually forgotten Fernando, and the vehement emotional image of Fernando's self-portrait shrinks when Augusta picks up the guitar he left behind, and tries to remember what she felt for the man who used to play it:

> For him who struck thy foreign string,
> I ween this heart has ceased to care;
> Then why dost thou such feelings bring
> To my sad spirit, old guitar?
>
> It is as if the warm sunlight
> In some deep glen should lingering stay,
> When clouds of tempest and of night
> Had wrapt the parent orb away.
>
> It is as if the glassy brook
> Should image still its willows fair,

Though years ago the woodman's stroke
Laid low in dust their gleaming hair.

Even so, guitar, thy magic tone
Has moved the tear and waked the sigh,
Has bid the ancient torrent flow
Although its very source is dry!
(#76, p. 80)

Augusta, in fact, feels none of the emotions Fernando attributes to her—neither hate, nor cruel triumph, nor tyrant's delight. Her tone is as subdued as Fernando's is violent, and it expresses a wondering, impersonal melancholy for one who is no more than a shadowy figure in her past. To complete the contrast and add yet another perspective, it is the girl Fernando left behind, and whom he deserted for Augusta, who remembers him vividly and is dying of heartbreak (#42, pp. 60–62). Written out of sequence and at different times, the Fernando poems show the broken lines of communication between people connected to one another. None of the participants in the drama knows what role the others have taken. Each speaker inhabits a subjective world only, and creates images of his or her own with which to people it.

Experiments in Form

So far we have had to do with internal and external portraits of character as they exist in different and sometimes widely separated poems. Different perspectives also appear in the same poem, however, to create a composite, multiple view of character or incident. "The Death of A. G. A." combines the objective, impersonal voice of an omniscient narrator with the involved, subjective voices of Douglas, Angelica, and Lord Eldred, who speak in self-contained monologues within the overall narrative frame. Even the lines alternate between ballad stanzas and rhyming tetrameter couplets. In several early, innovative poems, Brontë alternates even more radically between points of view to create a polyphonic effect out of a serial or slice-of-life technique. Different speakers appear in short lyrical or narrative sections, shifting the focus or center of the poem, and creating out of the whole a complex fabric of experience and perception.

One sequence runs from poems #48 to #57 in Hatfield's edition, and was written on both sides of a single manuscript sheet, with the date, March 1838, attached to poem #56.[6] The sequence concerns the assassination of Julius, although his death is not described or told. Time and scene change from section to section as point of view moves from involved to detached. The speakers are not identified, but the first is almost certainly Rosina at Julius's grave.

> Deep, deep down in the silent grave,
> With none to mourn above.
>
> ———
>
> Here, with my knee upon thy stone,
> I bid adieu to feelings gone;
> I leave with thee my tears and pain,
> And rush into the world again.
>
> ———
>
> O come again; what chains withhold
> The steps that used so fleet to be?
> Come, leave thy dwelling dank and cold
> Once more to visit me.
>
> (##48–50, p. 65)

In "Cold in the earth," when Rosina calls out to the dead Julius years later, we find the same mixture of love and determination not to forsake the world for that love.

In #51, the sequence moves from the immediate present into memory, as Rosina asks if Julius visited her in the fullness of summer. She is troubled because something is missing, now, from her symbol of life: "Summer skies will come again, / But *thou* wilt not be there" (#51, p. 65). We know from the Gondal story that Rosina was not with Julius when he died, so the next lyric, which tells of his funeral, is spoken by someone else. Moreover, the voice has changed; it is more objective and impersonal, and directs our attention less to Julius's funeral than to the state of the weather on the day it took place:

> How loud the storm sounds round the Hall!
> From arch to arch, from door to door,
> Pillar and roof and granite wall
> Rock like a cradle in its roar.

> That elm tree by the haunted well
> Greets no returning summer skies:
> Down with a rush the giant fell,
> And stretched athwart the path it lies.
>
> Hardly had passed the funeral train,
> So long delayed by wind and snow;
> And how they'll reach the house again
> To-morrow's dawn perhaps will show.
>   (#52, pp. 65–66)

The storm, however, can be read as a political allegory. Julius falls like a tree or giant man, and his death reverberates throughout the structure of Gondal society. The images objectify emotions that had been personal to Rosina and give them a more universal language and a more precise occasion. Rosina's lament, that Julius will not return with the summer, becomes the observer's comment on the fallen elm: it will greet "no returning summer skies." Interior emotion is attached more definitely to an exterior symbol.

In the next two lyrics (#53–#54), a voice seeks to comfort Rosina and rouse her from her lethargy. This could be one of Rosina's companions, the omniscient poet, or Rosina thinking to herself: "What use is it to slumber here, / Though the heart be sad and weary?" The day is dark, but the "mist may break when the sun is high, / And this soul forget its sorrow" (#53, p. 66). Poem #54 is written as a dialogue, probably between Rosina's thoughts and the spirit of nature. Rosina questions the evening, "why is thy light so sad?" She has been projecting her own sorrow onto her world, however, for nature answers her, "Hush; our smile is as ever glad, / But thy heart is growing old" (#54, p. 66). In #55, we move forward in time so that it is summer again. Rosina can draw strength from nature to recall "the fearful vision" of Julius's death. Heath and sky become the partners of her loneliness.

At this point in the sequence, the tone is again intensely personal and contemplative. Rosina has won a difficult spiritual peace. Chronology has shifted from the wintry grave to the funeral which preceded it and then to the summer which followed. In the next lyric Brontë changes perspective and tone dramatically. Julius is alive; the scene is that of his joint coronation with Gerald, whom Julius is already planning to kill.

The poem begins in an indefinite present and then moves into a flashback:

> The wide cathedral aisles are lone,
> The vast crowds vanished, every one;
> There can be naught beneath that dome
> But the cold tenants of the tomb.
>
> O look again, for still on high
> The lamps are burning gloriously;
> And look again, for still beneath
> A thousand thousand live and breathe.
>
> (#56, p. 67)

The narrator's memory fills the empty cathedral with the scene of the past coronation, and from his vantage point Gerald has already been betrayed, and Julius perhaps is dead, when he recalls "their awful vow." I quoted from the coronation scene in the last chapter, and as we saw, Julius is portrayed in negative, harsh terms. His eye is "imperious," his soul "perjured," and the smile that he cannot keep back as he thinks of his plot is a "bitter" one. Irony and sarcasm have replaced Rosina's romantic love in the poem's emotional center.

The sequence closes with another new speaker, and a very different involvement from Rosina's:

> O hinder me by no delay,
> My horse is weary of the way;
> And still his breast must stem the tide
> Whose waves are foaming far and wide.
> Leagues off I heard their thundering roar,
> As fast they burst upon the shore:
> A stronger steed than mine might dread
> To brave them in their boiling bed.
>
> Thus spoke the traveller, but in vain:
> The stranger would not turn away;
> Still clung she to his bridle rein,
> And still entreated him to stay.
>
> (#57, p. 68)

The poem presents difficulties: we do not know who the woman is or why the rider must make such haste. And there is no explicit connection between this scene and the story of Julius, Gerald, and Rosina. It is just possible that Brontë had concluded the Rosina-Julius sequence with poem #56, and included this poem on the same manuscript sheet because it was the handiest to her, or because she wanted to conserve paper. On the other hand, we have already dealt with unidentified speakers and abrupt transitions in the sequence, which, having to do with the death of kings, could well and logically include the portrait of an assassin. In the summer of 1838, shortly after she had finished the Rosina-Julius sequence, Brontë wrote "Douglas's Ride," in which Douglas has killed the Gondal ruler (unnamed) and is being hotly pursued. We know of Douglas as a conspirator and an outlaw. Eventually he murders Augusta Almeda, but is too severely wounded in the struggle with her to sustain the ordeal described in "Douglas's Ride." In that poem and in #57, the rider urges his weary horse to cross a dangerous patch of water; neither rider can afford the slightest delay. It is not certain, then, but it is very likely that #57 is spoken by Douglas, who has just killed the Gondal sovereign—not Gerald, whose death is arranged by Julius; but Julius himself.[7] Thus, the sequence that opens with the voice of Julius's lover closes with that of his killer. The narrative ends at a point of time just preceding its opening scene, with Julius dead and his body on its way to the grave where Rosina will mourn him.

The Rosina-Julius sequence, if it does not contain great poetry, shows a great imagination expanding the possibilities of what poetry can do. In its oblique, elliptical narrative, contrasting attitudes filter and divide the central episode of Julius's death. In another sequence, written shortly afterwards, in June 1838, the shift between internal and external perspectives results in one of Brontë's finest lyrics. It is an orchestrated whole that needs to be seen in its entirety, and for ease of reference I will include Hatfield's number for the individual poems or parts.

65

'Twas one of those dark, cloudy days
That sometimes come in summer's blaze,
When heaven drops not, when earth is still,
And deeper green is on the hill.

66

Lonely at her window sitting,
While the evening stole away;
Fitful winds, foreboding, flitting
Through a sky of cloudy grey.

67

There are two trees in a lonely field;
They breathe a spell to me;
A dreary thought their dark boughs yield,
All waving solemnly.

68

What is that smoke that ever still
Comes rolling down that dark brown hill?

69

Still as she looked the iron clouds
Would part, and sunlight shone between,
But drearily strange and pale and cold.

70

Away, away, resign me now
To scenes of gloom and thoughts of fear;
I trace the signal on thy brow,
Welcome at last, though once so drear.

71

It will not shine again;
Its sad course is done;
I have seen the last ray wane
Of the cold, bright sun.

72

None but one beheld him dying,
Parting with the parting day;
Winds of evening, sadly sighing,
Bore his soul from earth away.

73

Coldly, bleakly, drearily,
Evening died on Elbë's shore;

Winds were in the cloudy sky,
Sighing, mourning evermore.

74

Old Hall of Elbë, ruined, lonely now;
House to which the voice of life shall never more return;
Chambers roofless, desolate, where weeds and ivy grow;
Windows through whose broken arches the night-winds sadly mourn;
Home of the departed, the long-departed dead.

The chief figure—the woman at the window—is almost certainly
Augusta Almeda; the central event is the battle in which Alexander
Elbë died. This is referred to directly only in #68 and #72, but it
pervades the brooding atmosphere of the other poems. The sequence
uses montage to superimpose three scenes on each other: the landscape
outside Augusta's home on a cloudy summer evening, the battlefield,
and the ruins of old Elbë Hall. Each scene represents a different moment
of time. Augusta sits at her window in the immediate present. This
summer evening evokes memories of another summer evening when
Alexander was slain—and Brontë anticipates cinematic techniques by
making the setting sun dissolve into the dying Alexander. Finally, Elbë
Hall presents a lasting, timeless image of the battle's aftermath. The
hall became desolate with the death of Alexander, is "lonely now," and
will remain the same throughout the future.

Complementing the tripartite sense of time and place is a similar
modulation in point of view. The sequence as a whole comprises ten
poems, which in turn can be broken down into three groups of three
poems each and an epilogue. In each of the first two groups, point of
view shifts from omniscient narrator to Augusta; in the third group, the
movement is from Augusta to narrator, from limited to large-range
perspective, which in the epilogue encompasses the ruins of Elbë Hall.
In #65, that is, no human figure is present; from an overview the
narrator describes "one of those dark, cloudy days." In #66, the view
narrows to a woman sitting lonely "at *her* window." In #67, we enter
into the thoughts of the woman herself: "There are two trees in a lonely
field; / They breathe a spell to *me*." At this point memory replaces
landscape, so that the smoke rolling down the hill in #68 is the scene in
Augusta's mind as well as the expanded vision of the narrator. In #69,

Augusta is described in the third person again: "Still as she looked"; and in #70, she speaks in the first person: "Away, away, resign me now." Thus, though not identical, the pattern of the second group parallels and repeats that of the first. Point of view concentrates and becomes more individualized as it changes from an unidentified narrator's observations, to third person description of character, to first person utterance.

The third group reverses the pattern. In #71, Augusta speaks in the first person: "I have seen the last ray wane / Of the cold, bright sun." The next poem describes Augusta from the outside, in the third person: "None but one beheld him dying." Poem #73 and the epilogue expand further outward as the narrator describes the ruins of Elbë Hall. There are circles within circles, in effect, along a graduated scale from Augusta's consciousness to the narrator's.

For a nineteen-year-old, self-taught writer, it is a very considerable achievement. Instead of the devices which we normally find in Victorian poetry, such as authorial comment or discursive exposition of meaning, Brontë uses a series of impressions, related images, and associated scenes to produce an effect very similar to that of the stream-of-consciousness novel. We are given the fragments of a crisis in bits and pieces of memory and perception until the final description of the old hall. It is itself a ruin that was once whole, and a collective image that joins the house from which Augusta looks out her window and the battlefield she sees in her mind. Almost a decade before *Wuthering Heights,* evidently, Brontë had already learned to create and control her own technique.

The Major Themes of the Poetry

The major concern of Emily Brontë's poetry is a quest for freedom and for self-fulfillment in a force or principle larger than the self. This over-riding theme involves several thematic groups or motifs, as Brontë deals with the threats to freedom, with the different roles of nature in the liberating process, and with an inner division between the rival claims of nature and imagination. Brontë's thematic concerns cut across the division between Gondal and non-Gondal poems, and the evolution of her ideas approximates only roughly the chronology of her writing.

The later, personal poems show her increasingly engaged in the nature of her imagination and the liberating effects of its creative power; but the theme of the prison, for instance, appears throughout her poetry, both early and late. In a number of related poems, Brontë engages in a thematic dialogue or debate between rival positions—in much the same way that she presented character from more than one perspective. The thematic structure of her poems, however, as opposed to their chronological sequence, is that of a pilgrimage, in which we follow the soul's ascent from captivity to liberty; from prison, and the isolated self, to freedom and union with the universe.

Theme of the Prison: The Soul in Hell. The darkest moments in Brontë's poetry—its spiritual bottom—take place in prison, or in the prisonlike condition of the exile and outcast. As we saw in the poem, "A little while, a little while," Brontë thought of the school room as a prison, barring her from the free life of imagination. She has only a short respite from her tasks, and laments,

> Could I have lingered but an hour
> It well had paid a week of toil,
> But truth has banished fancy's power;
> I hear my dungeon bars recoil[.]
> (#92, p. 95)

Julius Brenzaida is imprisoned for moral reasons; and his dungeon, in the "Southern College," is a sort of school room and enforces the notion of instruction as confinement. But a large number of other Gondalans find themselves in prison, and for reasons that are not always clear—Augusta Almeda, Fernando, Gerald Exina, one of the Glenedens; while others, like Angelica, Alfred, and Douglas, are doomed to a prisonlike perpetual exile. While we can infer that most of these are victims of the shifting fortunes of Gondal politics, the frequency with which imprisonment or exile occurs in the Gondal story suggests that Emily Brontë saw it as an inescapable or ever-threatening condition of life.

For Brontë, who loved to make wide-ranging rambles on the moors, and for whom, as Charlotte says, liberty was the breath of life, there could be no darker or more ominous symbol than the prison.[8] Its immediate effect, of course, is to cut the prisoner off from nature: Brontë cannot return to the familiar fields around her home; Julius cannot sail with his companions on the open seas to Gaaldine. We see the effects of this separation in another Gondalan, identified only as M. A., who is imprisoned in the Northern College. Though he knows that the moon is shining, she will neither "wax nor wane" for him in his cell; and in fact, he is one of a number of psychic or mental casualties, wounded because prison keeps them from the natural cycle and its restorative powers:

> For this constant darkness is wasting the gladness,
> Fast wasting the gladness of life away:
> It gathers up thoughts akin to madness
> That never would cloud the world of day.
>
> (#189, p. 235)

Fernando De Samara also fears that imprisonment will "kill" his mind and drive him insane (#133, p. 139). Gleneden must ask the prison guard if it is winter: "Have the woods I left so lovely / Lost their robes of tender green?" (#63, p. 72). Gleneden has lost all touch with seasonal time—winter has come and gone—and lives instead in the feverish atmosphere of his dream, in which he stabs Julius to death. The effects of her imprisonment have totally disoriented Iernë, who can no longer tell day from night, or sun from moon:

> Iernë's eyes were glazed and dim
> When the castle bell tolled one.
> She looked around her dungeon grim;
> The grating cast a doubtful gleam;
> 'Twas one cloud-saddened cold moon-beam.
> Iernë gazed as in a dream
> And thought she saw the sun.
>
> She thought it was the break of day,
> The night had been so long.
>
> (#46, p. 64)

The prison is the dark night of her mind: it distorts reality and deranges thoughts.

Even when the prisoner has been released, the mental wounds of imprisonment can remain, as in the anguished speaker of the poem which begins, "O God of heaven! the dream of horror, / The frightful dream is over now" (#15, pp. 40–43). It is not over, though. He carries the horror of his imprisonment within him, in feelings that he cannot quell, in memories that are more vividly present than the sea and sky he looks upon. And "even now too horribly," his despair returns.

Although nominally more free than the prisoner, the exile, shut out from home and from the early associations that made life worthwhile, also suffers deep emotional wounds. The most desperate of them, Fernando, escapes from prison only to wander a bleak moor, where he commits suicide (#85, pp. 85–87). Alfred's ghost, unable to rest in England, haunts Aspin Castle (#154, pp. 175–79). Another exile, named Claudia, lives in two places at once: fettered in body to a foreign soil, her soul wanders the distant landscape of her home (#102, pp. 109–10). But there are those too who live in mental, rather than physical, exile, who are exiled by their very natures or perceptions. The disillusioned youth of "I am the only being whose doom," as we saw, rejects all of mankind. In the following poem, which has the initials A. A., the speaker's perception alienates her from life itself, and causes her to identify instead with the forces of death—winter and decay:

> Fall, leaves, fall; die, flowers, away;
> Lengthen night and shorten day;
> Every leaf speaks bliss to me
> Fluttering from the autumn tree.
> I shall smile when wreaths of snow
> Blossom where the rose should grow;
> I shall sing when night's decay
> Ushers in a drearier day.
>   (#79, p. 82)

Her song celebrates a cosmic death, and completes her isolation from life.

In Emily Brontë's poetry, exile or imprisonment symbolizes the state of the soul when it cannot pass beyond the confining limits of its own existence, and when it can only glimpse but not participate in a larger existence, a spiritual or universal force that is its true identity. In Brontë's cosmic scheme, the prison cell of the self-reduced-to-itself is the equivalent of hell or damnation, the point furthest away from salvation. We see this clearly in *Wuthering Heights,* when Catherine Earnshaw, exiled from the Heights, tells Nelly Dean and Heathcliff that "the thing that irks me most is this shattered prison, after all. I'm tired, tired of being enclosed here. I'm wearying to escape into that glorious world, and to be always there; not seeing it dimly through tears, and yearning for it through the walls of an aching heart; but really with it and in it."[9] What Catherine yearns for is not heaven in any traditional sense, but an expansion of being in which the self shares one consciousness or existence with all things.

Nature Pro and Contra: Expanded Vision or a Veil. The Gondal prisoners suffer a derangement of their senses or fall into madness because they are cut off from nature and its restorative cycles. Catherine Earnshaw, on the other hand, is imprisoned in her body, by nature itself, which throws a screen between her soul and the glorious world she yearns for. As a larger principle of life, nature releases the soul from its confinement to itself, but as the physical world it presents to the soul only what is material and visible, while the soul yearns for the invisible and the spiritual. Brontë herself was drawn both to the earth and to something beyond it, and her opposing views of nature engage her in one of the central conflicts of her poetry, as nature becomes the middle stage between the soul in hell and the soul in paradise.

In one of her earliest poems, Brontë identifies nature explicitly as a liberating force, releasing the soul from prison:

> High waving heather, 'neath stormy blasts bending,
> Midnight and moonlight and bright shining stars;
> Darkness and glory rejoicingly blending,
> Earth rising to heaven and heaven descending,
> Man's spirit away from its drear dungeon sending,
> Bursting the fetters and breaking the bars.
> (#5, p. 31)

While confined in the school room that was like a prison to her, Brontë could derive comfort and sustenance from the memory of the natural scene around her home:

> The mute bird sitting on the stone,
> The dank moss dripping from the wall,

> The garden-walk with weeds o'ergrown,
> I love them—how I love them all!
>   (#92, p. 94)

In "There should be no despair for you," humanity and nature share the
same destiny, as Brontë sees man's fate repeated and enlarged in the
encompassing cycles of nature. Winds sigh as her listener is sighing,
and though autumn's leaves now lie under the snow, "Yet they revive,
and from their fate / Your fate cannot be parted" (#122, p. 131). Even
when the wintry landscape is seen as the death of nature, barren of
flowers and buds, it can recall memories and yearnings of spring that
breathe upon her heart "A calm and softening spell" (#94, p. 98). And
as a necessary phase of nature's cycle, winter has its own beauty. Its
stillness and quiet, before the storms of spring, allow the soul rest and
expansion, so that Brontë loves

> December's smile
> As much as July's golden beam;
> Then let us sit and watch the while
> The blue ice curdling on the stream.
>   (#93, p. 97)

While she is in prison, Augusta's heart is thrilled at the sight of a
wreath of snow on her window bars; a sign from the outside world, it
will comfort and sustain her (#39, pp. 57–58).

Brontë's celebration of nature, in "I see around me tombstones grey"
(#149, pp. 166–67), does not blind her to the wounds of "Time and
Death and Mortal pain"; the graveyard reminds her that life is held only
to be lost. Yet the earth's children, she says, would rather share with the
earth "A mutual immortality" than be among the blessed in heaven,
where they would not belong. "We would not leave our native home /
For *any* world beyond the Tomb." In the straightforward nature lyric
which begins, "I've been wandering in the greenwoods" (#128, pp.
135–36), Brontë shows that she responds to the particular things of the
earth—not nature in the abstract, but "the pale primrose," the crystal
fountain, "the fair enamelled ground." Cherishing the landscapes of her
earliest associations and memories, Brontë found in nature what George
Eliot calls "the mother tongue of our imagination."[10]

Nature, however, releases the imagination from one prison, that of the isolated self, only to enclose it in another prison, the barrier of the physical world. From this view, imagination or the soul is like a caged bird that only death can release from the prison of life:

> But let me think that if to-day
> It pines in cold captivity,
> To-morrow both shall soar away,
> Eternally, entirely Free.
>
> (#144, p. 162)

As Brontë's celebration of nature expresses itself in a strong zest for life, so her sense of nature as a prison releases a corresponding death wish. "There's nothing lovely here," she says in one poem; "the happiest story . . . closes with the tomb." One should not mourn the dead, but the living:

> So, if a tear, when thou art dying,
> Should haply fall from me,
> It is but that my soul is sighing
> To go and rest with thee.
>
> (#136, p. 142)

Only with death, Brontë writes in "Aye, there it is! It wakes tonight," shall the "prisoned soul" arise: "The dungeon mingle with the mould— / The captive with the skies" (#148, p. 165).

The dualism which opposes the spiritual world of imagination to the physical world of objective reality is most explicit in a poem which Brontë entitled "To Imagination":

> When weary with the long day's care,
> And earthly change from pain to pain,
> And lost, and ready to despair,
> Thy kind voice calls me back again—
> O my true friend, I am not lone
> While thou canst speak with such a tone!
>
> So hopeless is the world without,
> The world within I doubly prize;

Thy world where guile and hate and doubt
And cold suspicion never rise;
Where thou and I and Liberty
Have undisputed sovereignty.

What matters it that all around
Danger and grief and darkness lie,
If but within our bosom's bound
We hold a bright unsullied sky,
Warm with ten thousand mingled rays
Of suns that know no winter days?

Reason indeed may oft complain
For Nature's sad reality,
And tell the suffering heart how vain
Its cherished dreams must always be;
And Truth may rudely trample down
The flowers of Fancy newly blown.

But thou art ever there to bring
The hovering visions back and breathe
New glories o'er the blighted spring
And call a lovelier life from death,
And whisper with a voice divine
Of real worlds as bright as thine.

(#174, pp. 205–206)

The poem expresses virtually a complete rejection of nature, "the world without," which is no longer the sustaining earth, but a "sad reality." The darkness of what is forces the imagination to its own inward light of what ought to be. Imagination, in effect, creates a spiritual image of nature, with "bright unsullied sky," to compensate for the flawed reality.

In "A Day Dream," Brontë portrays herself as a sullen guest at the marriage of May and June. The freshness and hope of spring are an unreal appearance, for "When winter comes again, / Where will these bright things be?" Death is inescapable, and "The birds that now so blithely sing" will change into famished specters.

> "And why should we be glad at all?
> The leaf is hardly green
> Before a token of the fall
> Is on its surface seen."
> (#170, p. 199)

The soul cannot look forward to a "mutual immortality" with the earth, as in "I see around me tombstones grey," but is compelled to go inward to imagination. A vision comes to Brontë of spirits which tell her that nature is a veil the mind must see through:

> "To Thee the world is like a tomb,
> A desert's naked shore;
> To us, in unimagined bloom,
> It brightens more and more.
>
> "And could we lift the veil and give
> One brief glimpse to thine eye
> Thou would'st rejoice for those that live,
> Because they live to die."
> (#170, p. 200)

Death is final only for those who see by the light of nature rather than that of imagination.

The death wish in Brontë's poetry seems to express her frustration at being unable to experience in its fullness a spiritual existence which came to her at intermittent moments, often very powerfully, but which nature and her physical existence stood in the way of. Significantly, it was at night, when nature is asleep or dark, that her mind was most alive and could see most clearly, and in several key poems on the imagination, the opposition between the inward and the outward worlds takes the form of this duality of perception by night and by day.

In "Aye, there it is! It wakes to-night," a strong wind sweeps "the world aside," and awakens the soul or imagination, which becomes a wind-like force itself as it merges with the universal principle of life:

> And thou art now a spirit pouring
> Thy presence into all—

> The essence of the Tempest's roaring
> And of the Tempest's fall—
>
> A universal influence
> From Thine own influence free;
> A principle of life, intense,
> Lost to mortality.
>   (#148, p. 165)

When the earth goes dark, in "How clear she shines" (#157, pp. 184–85), the mind can travel outward to heaven, where the dream of what ought to be replaces the grim reality of what is. Brontë's rejection of nature is emphatic:

> The world is going—Dark world, adieu!
> Grim world, go hide thee till the day;
> The heart thou canst not all subdue
> Must still resist if thou delay!
>
> Thy love I will not, will not share;
> Thy hatred only wakes a smile;
> Thy griefs may wound—thy wrongs may tear,
> But, oh, thy lies shall ne'er beguile!

In contrast, imagination or "Fancy" is her "Fairy love."

Admittedly, the oppression which Brontë feels in "How clear she shines" is located as much in man's inhumanity to man as in nature. But it is nature itself that opposes the mind in "Ah! why, because the dazzling sun" (#184, pp. 225–27). At night, under the stars, the mind feels the spiritual force which joins all things into one existence; with the coming of day, the sun reveals to the eye the multiplicity of things, and creates the prison of separateness.[11] The cycle of night and day is that of paradise found and paradise lost:

> Thought followed thought—star followed star
> Through boundless regions on,
> While one sweet influence, near and far,
> Thrilled through and proved us one.

Why did the morning rise to break
So great, so pure a spell,
And scorch with fire the tranquil cheek
Where your cool radiance fell?

Blood-red he rose, and arrow-straight
His fierce beams struck my brow:
The soul of Nature sprang elate,
But mine sank sad and low!

The rise of the outward world triggers the decline of the world within.

Imagination in these latter poems is Brontë's all-in-all; in "O thy bright eyes must answer now" (#176, pp. 208–209), it is her "God of Visions," the "radiant angel" that will defend her against the judgment of reason. But she was not without a sense of its inadequacies either; and as we have seen, her concept of nature alternates between that of a sustaining mother and a hostile prison. As Herbert Dingle remarks, one might read Brontë's "poems on the Earth and pronounce her a pagan, while from the mystical poems the conclusion might be drawn that the Earth meant nothing to her."[12] And Inga-Stina Ewbank speaks of Brontë's vision as encompassing "the paradoxical opposites of an attachment to, even an identification with, earth and a yearning away from it."[13] Even in the poem "To Imagination," which champions the world within against the world without, Brontë cannot trust imagination's "phantom bliss."

Brontë knew that to divorce imagination from nature would threaten an important source of its creative power; and in "O Dream, where art thou now," she mourns the loss of organic unity between the inner and the outer worlds:

The sun-beam and the storm,
The summer-eve divine,
The silent night of solemn calm,
The full moon's cloudless shine,

Were once entwined with thee,
But now with weary pain,

> Lost vision! 'tis enough for me—
> Thou canst not shine again.
>   (#86, p. 87)

Here it is not a question of unity between the soul and something beyond nature, but one of unity between the soul and nature. Separation from nature is the soul's loss of vision.

The soul's or the mind's dependence on nature is elaborated in "Shall Earth no more inspire thee" (#147, pp. 163–64), in which the earth calls the imagination back from its "useless roving" in an unsubstantial realm. The earth asserts its "magic power" to give pleasure, "To drive . . . griefs away"; and the heaven which the imagination has been seeking outside or beyond nature is in fact all around it on the earth:

> Few hearts to mortals given
> On earth so wildly pine;
> Yet none would ask a heaven
> More like this Earth than thine.
>
> Then let my winds caress thee;
> Thy comrade let me be—
> Since nought beside can bless thee,
> Return and dwell with me.

The theme, the intimation of a paradise on earth, is similar to what we found in "I see around me tombstones grey," where Brontë speaks in her own voice. "Then let my winds caress thee": the wind is both the spiritualized or invisible being of nature and a familiar Romantic symbol for the imagination. In "The Night-Wind" (#140, pp. 146–47), it mediates between heaven and earth: "It told me Heaven was glorious, / And sleeping Earth was fair." And it reveals not only the physical beauty of nature, but the spiritual life within "the world without":

> "The thick leaves in my murmur
> Are rustling like a dream,
> And all their myriad voices
> Instinct with spirit seem."

Brontë attempts to resist nature's call and to separate her human feelings from its music, but the wind asserts their companionship: "Have we not been from childhood friends? / Have I not loved thee long?" There will be time enough for their separation when she is in the tomb.

Chronologically, "The Night-Wind" precedes those poems—"To Imagination," "A Day Dream"—in which the division between the inner and outer worlds is most acute. Thematically, it looks beyond the division and anticipates reconciliation: Brontë's moments of vision, in which imagination penetrates to the spiritual life within nature and releases its own highest power.

The Imagination Finds God. One of Brontë's most difficult and philosophical poems, "Enough of Thought, Philosopher" (#181, pp. 220–21), is a dialogue between a man who sees only the divisions and conflicts of life and a "Seer" who has found life's unity. The first wishes for death because "Three Gods within this little frame / Are warring night and day." So as long as he is alive, aware of himself, he will not be free of their struggle. The Seer corrects him. The three are not three but one, and exist as such precisely where the man is standing now:

> "I saw a Spirit standing, Man,
> Where thou dost stand—an hour ago;
> And round his feet, three rivers ran
> Of equal depth and equal flow—
>
> "A Golden stream, and one like blood,
> And one like Sapphire, seemed to be,
> But where they joined their triple flood
> It tumbled in an inky sea.
>
> "The Spirit bent his dazzling gaze
> Down on that Ocean's gloomy night,
> Then—kindling all with sudden blaze,
> The glad deep sparkled wide and bright—
> White as the sun; far, far more fair
> Than the divided sources were!"

It is the "dazzling gaze," the light of imagination, that kindles night into day and finds unity within division.

The most dramatic of these transfigurations occurs in the poem, "Julian M. and A. G. Rochelle." The setting, significantly, is a prison, Brontë's symbol for hell. Imagination changes it to paradise; the starting point of the soul's quest contains its end. A young Gondal woman, A. G. Rochelle, has been captured during the civil wars and suffers an extreme form of confinement, in fetters and within triple walls. Although she defies her adversary by saying that death will free her, she goes on to tell of a vision that allows her to experience life at its most intense. The hereafter, and all that the mind hopes for in the hereafter, occurs now:

"He comes with western winds, with evening's wandering airs,
With that clear dusk of heaven that brings the thickest stars;
Winds take a pensive tone, and stars a tender fire,
And visions rise and change which kill me with desire—

"Desire for nothing known in my maturer years
When joy grew mad with awe at counting future tears;
When, if my spirit's sky was full of flashes warm,
I knew not whence they came, from sun or thunderstorm;

"But first a hush of peace, a soundless calm descends;
The struggle of distress and fierce impatience ends;
Mute music soothes my breast—unuttered harmony
That I could never dream till earth was lost to me.

"Then dawns the Invisible, the Unseen its truth reveals;
My outward sense is gone, my inward essence feels—
Its wings are almost free, its home, its harbour found;
Measuring the gulf it stoops and dares the final bound!"
                                                    (#190, pp. 238–39)

The vision is brought to Rochelle, as Brontë's was, by the night-wind, or through the medium of nature, which then becomes transparent, a glass that allows the imagination to see the invisible. It is not the longed-for death, then, but the mind's capacity for visionary experience that releases the soul to its mutual immortality with the soul of nature.

At once, Rochelle achieves a peace that passes understanding and reaches the emotional summit of life. But hers is an experience in which intensity makes up for duration, and it cannot last. Thus, the agony is dreadful when Rochelle's separate identity reasserts itself, and she becomes conscious again of the limits of her individuality:

> "When the ear begins to hear and the eye begins to see;
> When the pulse begins to throb, the brain to think again,
> The soul to feel the flesh and the flesh to feel the chain!"

The moment of vision creates one world, without distinction between the inward and the outward. Their state of division begins again when the eye takes over from the mind the power of seeing. But if the bliss is not permanent, neither is the agony. The vision returns each night, so that if, in nature's cycle, the soul must "feel the flesh," it will also happen, in the answering spiritual cycle, that the flesh becomes all soul.

Rochelle's vision is a later version and clarification of the night vision of such poems as "Ah! why, because the dazzling sun."[14] There the mind travels outward from multiplicity to celestial unity with the stars: heaven is above, apart from the earth. Rochelle's salvation comes to her—it is as close as Catherine Earnshaw's spirit is to Heathcliff, when he sees it hardly more than three feet away from him.[15] In "No coward soul is mine," written shortly after "Julian M. and A. G. Rochelle," on January 2, 1846, there is no distance at all between the soul and its paradise. Brontë calls upon God, and finds God within herself:

> No coward soul is mine
> No trembler in the world's storm-troubled sphere
> I see Heaven's glories shine
> And Faith shines equal arming me from Fear
>
> O God within my breast
> Almighty ever-present Deity
> Life, that in me hast rest
> As I Undying Life, have power in Thee[.]
>
> (#191, p. 243)

God is "ever-present" to Emily now, and exists within her as a power. The Brontës were widely read in the Romantic poets, who identified the creative imagination as a power. Coleridge, in his Dejection Ode, calls it "This beautiful and beauty-making power." The romantic imagination is a concept of perception as a shaping force upon what it perceives; activated by joy or love, the imagination becomes one with its object. Brontë's deity, both transcendent above and immanent in all things, is the power of perception:

> With wide-embracing love
> Thy spirit animates eternal years
> Pervades and broods above,
> Changes, sustains, dissolves, creates and rears
>
> Though Earth and moon were gone
> And suns and universes ceased to be
> And thou wert left alone
> Every Existence would exist in thee[.]
>   (#191, p. 243)

As we shall see, Catherine Earnshaw speaks in virtually the same terms about Heathcliff. Because the "thee" that is the source of all existence exists in Brontë herself, we can say that she reached a point of vision, at the end of her writing, from which the inward world no longer opposes the world without, but contains all that is essential in that world.

But in the universal center of being which Brontë has found, the reverse is equally true. Thus, in the last poem of Hatfield's edition, the outward world contains all that is essential to the world within:[16]

> Often rebuked, yet always back returning
>   To those first feelings that were born with me,
> And leaving busy chase of wealth and learning
>   For idle dreams of things which cannot be:
>
> To-day, I will seek not the shadowy region;
>   Its unsustaining vastness waxes drear;
> And visions rising, legion after legion,
>   Bring the unreal world too strangely near.

I'll walk, but not in old heroic traces,
   And not in paths of high morality,
And not among the half-distinguished faces,
   The clouded forms of long-past history.

I'll walk where my own nature would be leading:
   It vexes me to choose another guide:
Where the gray flocks in ferny glens are feeding;
   Where the wild wind blows on the mountain side.

What have those lonely mountains worth revealing?
   More glory and more grief than I can tell:
The earth that wakes *one* human heart to feeling
   Can centre both the worlds of Heaven and Hell.
                        (pp. 255–56)

Brontë rejects the "unreal" vision that is divorced from the physical world, and locates or discovers her imaginative powers, her "own nature," in external nature. The earth that wakes and the heart that responds encompass the universe.

This chapter has dealt with Brontë's poetic themes as a quest of the soul or the imagination from the narrow cell of the isolated self, to the larger but still restricted world of nature, to the universal sphere where the self both becomes and unites with the principle of all being. To be sure, Brontë did not write a *Divine Comedy,* or arrange her poems in a systematic structure like Dante's. She was a lyric, not an epic poet. Her poems record various moods or states of feeling—the moments of despair, conflict, and bliss that went into her manuscript books as she imagined or experienced them. Suddenly, however, after "No coward soul is mine," the record stops. As we saw in her biography, she wrote practically nothing for the last two-and-a-half years of her life. It is not likely that she had lost the power to write, though it is possible that it was no longer necessary for her to write, because she had come to the end of her quest. Was she waiting for death to release her utterly to what lies beyond this life? Her mind, in those final years, as we saw, remains unknown to us. On the other hand, Brontë seems to imply that her quest—or her mission as a poet—was not over, even when the ascent from hell to heaven has been made. After all, the mountains of her native land still had "More glory and more grief than [she] can tell." In that case, like Yeats in "The Circus Animals' Desertion," in order to go on telling, Brontë would have to descend the ladder she had climbed and begin again at the bottom. She would not know, of course, how little time was left her to do that.

Chapter Four

The Essays in French

During her nine-month stay in Brussels, from February to November 1842, Emily Brontë wrote only three poems, two of which were not finished until after her return to Haworth. The years immediately before and after the Brussels episode were, in contrast, fruitful and prolific. The difference underlines the fact that Emily went to the Pensionnat Héger to study, to prepare herself to teach in the Brontë's projected school; and it reminds us that away from home Emily's spirits and creative energies did not flourish. Brussels was doubly foreign to both the Brontës in being French-speaking and Catholic, but whereas Charlotte welcomed the change, Emily endured it. Provincial, suspicious of the Belgians and their customs, reserved by nature, Emily withdrew into herself and survived what must have been a hard and bitter time for her by determining, as the Hansons say, "to make the school pay, in learning, for the unhappiness it was causing."[1]

Yet the Brussels experience provides us with a rare instance of seeing Brontë's mind up close. Charlotte and Emily had gone to Brussels to learn French. Their teacher, M. Héger, recognized their intellectual capacities, and taking into account their age—in their twenties, they were older than their fellow-pupils—he taught them by the method he used for his more advanced students. This consisted of reading and analyzing masterpieces of French literature, and then writing essays on a similar subject to that of their reading, in their own manner, but drawing upon the excellencies of style they had learned. Brontë objected to the plan at first, fearing it would cause them to lose "all originality of thought and expression."[2] But she made, apparently, rapid progress in French, and was able to express her views and to use her creative techniques in the essay form in a foreign language. Seven of her essays, ranging from two hundred to eight hundred words, survive: "The Cat," "Portrait of King Harold Before the Battle of Hastings," "Lettre," "Filial Love," "Letter from One Brother to Another," "The

Butterfly," and "The Palace of Death." With so much of Brontë's life closed to us, and most of her prose destroyed, these have a special importance in allowing us a glimpse of her thoughts and feelings without the masks that she used in her poetry and her novel—or with the mask much thinner; it is never certain when Brontë is speaking in her own voice. Fannie Ratchford, the critic who has probably done the most to dissociate Brontë's literature from her personal life, thinks that the essays in French "are in a very real sense autobiographical, sketching the fullest and clearest self-portrait we have of Emily."[3] In fact, the picture of her which emerges from the essays—from their themes and concerns—matches the Emily Brontë we know from the poems and *Wuthering Heights,* but there are deviations, too, attitudes that do not appear, in the same way, anywhere else in her writings.

In the "Portrait of Harold" (*Essays in French,* pp. 11–12), we find the familiar Brontëan image of the soul in prison about to be released by death. As king, Harold is kept prisoner by his court, by the political system and chain of power of which he is at once the head and the victim: ". . . of all his people he is the least free, a creature without courage to act or think for himself, knowing that all around him are trying to confuse his soul in a labyrinth of follies and vices, conscious that it is to their interest that he should be blinded, kept powerless to raise a hand without the direction of his ministers, and knowing that his body is actually a prisoner, with his kingdom for prison and his subjects for guards." In his palace, that is, he would be entirely passive, dependent on the machinations of his ministers and the pleasures of his people. But the battlefield, "without palace, without ministers, without courtiers, without pomp, without luxury," has transformed Harold from king to hero, a national symbol upon whose fate and strength rest the safety and existence of his people. His emotions purified by the importance of his cause, dealing with essential things and not distractions, Harold becomes larger than life: "A soul divine, visible to his fellow men as to his Creator, gleams in his eyes." He is beyond the reach of any mere mortal power. "Death alone can gain victory over his arms. To her he is ready to yield, for Death's touch is to the hero what the striking off his chains is to the slave."

Brontë's national prejudices, of course, show through the lines of the portrait. The Anglo-Saxon king will be overcome by the invading

French and slain, but he will not have been defeated by them. He has won his victory in the expansion of his soul to heroic form and in his courage before the inescapable. The historical Harold is thus made more idealistic, more mythical, than are the flawed rulers of Brontë's myth—the tyrannical and self-willed Julius and Augusta. In the Gondal wars, Brontë portrays violence realistically and shows its awful murderousness; in the "Portrait of Harold," she tends almost to exalt it, in that the prospect of violence allows Harold to find his soul and release a moral energy. Ultimately, he views the battle, not as between two armies of men, but as between himself and Death. His portrait provides us, I think, with the rare occasion of seeing Brontë too moved by her own subject to examine it.

She has much more control in two later essays which also deal with conflict and violence, "A Letter from One Brother to Another" and "The Butterfly." In the first, two brothers have had an angry quarrel and have not seen each other for ten years. The writer of the letter has never forgotten the vow of eternal hatred which they swore, but now, worn out by his wanderings, he has returned home. The house is lit but silent, and as the man searches the rooms, the narrative becomes tense with the expectation of the brothers' encounter.

> I crossed the room, the corridor, the anterooms, without meeting anyone and found myself in the library, once our common retreat, the place reserved for the thousand memories that a century of absence could not efface. While in the flickering light of the fire I was looking at the pictures on the walls, the rows of books beneath, and all the familiar objects which surrounded me, something in the room stirred. It was a big dog which rose from a dark corner and approached to examine the stranger. He did not find a stranger. He was glad to see me and showed his joy by the most expressive caresses, but I pushed him away, because he was yours.
>
> (*Essays in French,* p. 16)

Immediately he repents, and ends the letter by asking his brother for forgiveness. But the hatred was so ingrained in him that even on what is presumably a mission of reconciliation, and surrounded by objects that recall their youth together, his instinctive response is an aggressive one. The action gives his character a psychological truth that the portrait of

Harold lacks. The man who has lived for ten years in a state of mental violence against his brother acts violently at the first sign of him.

In "The Butterfly" (*Essays in French,* pp. 17–19), the most important and metaphysical of the essays, Brontë sees violence as a universal law of nature. She describes herself walking on the edge of a forest, in a state of deep spiritual crisis. The harmony and beauty of nature seem to her to be only a "semblance," an illusion which clashes against her own desolate mood, in which "the world of imagination suffers the blight of winter," and "existence becomes a barren desert . . . without hope of rest or shelter." Hearing a nightingale sing, she rebukes it: "Is it to guide a bullet to your breast or a boy to your little ones that you are singing so loud and clear?" The nightingale is trapped in a murderous scheme of existence, for "All creation is equally insane." All life hunts and is hunted: "There are those flies playing above the stream, swallows and fish diminishing their number each minute: these will become in their turn, the prey of some tyrant of air or water; and man for his amusement or for his needs will kill their murderers. Nature is an inexplicable puzzle, life exists on a principle of destruction; every creature must be the relentless instrument of death to the others, or himself cease to live." And man, too, who kills and devours, dies and "is devoured—that's his whole story."

Nothing in the poems or even *Wuthering Heights* quite equals the stark disillusionment of "The Butterfly," in which nature shows a senseless and rapacious struggle for existence. It is very doubtful that Brontë knew of the scientific research that would culminate in the theory of natural selection. Yet she anticipates by eight years Tennyson's "Nature, red in tooth and claw"; and she is seventeen years ahead of *The Origin of Species,* in which Darwin draws the same contrast between the happy appearance of nature and its underlying, real violence. "We behold the face of nature bright with gladness," Darwin writes, "we often see superabundance of food; we do not see or we forget that the birds which are idly singing round us mostly live on insects or seeds, and are thus constantly destroying life; or we forget how largely these songsters, or their eggs, or their nestlings, are destroyed by birds and beasts of prey."[4] Like Darwin's, Brontë's vision is both microscopic and telescopic. She sees the destruction occurring before her at the moment, and the long chain of destruction of which it is a link.

Brontë may have been drawing upon her memories of *King Lear,*
particularly Gloucester's chilling image of senseless universal violence:
"As flies to wanton boys, are we to the gods, / They kill us for their
sport."[5] Much closer to her in time is Keats, whose verse "Epistle to
John Hamilton Reynolds" ends with a startling view of life as a
relentless struggle for existence. Seated by the sea, where all was quiet,
he should have been happy, but

> I saw
> Too far into the sea, where every maw
> The greater on the less feeds evermore—
> But I saw too distinct into the core
> Of an eternal fierce destruction.

Though he leaves the scene, the vision follows him:

> Still do I that most fierce destruction see,—
> The Shark at savage prey,—the Hawk at pounce,—
> The gentle Robin, like a Pard or Ounce,
> Ravening a worm.[6]

It is a horrid mood, Keats says, from which he will take refuge in a new
romance. Brontë, for whom there is yet no escape, moves closer to the
destructive center. Picking a pretty flower, she finds an ugly caterpillar
hiding in its petals, "and already they were drawing up and withering.
'Sad image of the earth and its inhabitants!' I exclaimed. 'This worm
lives only by destroying the plant which protects him; why was he
created and why was man created?'" All life is meaningless, and God
should have destroyed the world and annihilated man "on the day of his
first sin." To show her contempt for life, she throws the flower to the
ground and crushes the insect with her foot.

She thus becomes an agent of the violence she condemns.[7] But the
next moment she sees a butterfly fluttering through the trees, and her
perspective changes radically. Her imagination had been dead; now an
inner voice reveals to her that, "as the ugly caterpillar is the beginning
of the splendid butterfly, this globe is the embryo of a new heaven and
of a new earth whose meagerest beauty infinitely surpasses mortal

imagination." The vision reconciles her to God and nature and to the
suffering which God inflicts on life: ". . . each suffering of our unhappy
nature is only a seed for that divine harvest which will be gathered when
sin having spent its last drop of poison, death having thrown its last
dart, both will expire on the funeral pyre of a universe in flame, and will
leave their former victims to an eternal realm of happiness and glory."
Brontë has passed from the mystic's dark night of the soul, when she
was conscious only of nature's senseless struggle for existence, to a
beatific revelation that harmonizes and explains all.

Butterflies, of course, are a symbol of rebirth and the ancient Greek
symbol for the soul—the caterpillar (the body) dies to release its higher
and more beautiful existence.[8] Brontë uses the symbol in its traditional
sense, but expands on it to make the caterpillar stand for the state of
perception with which she begins the essay. As the caterpillar destroys
the beautiful flower, so Brontë's disillusioned or contemptuous mood
infects the scene before her, and denying the reality of beauty, it sees
only nature's relentless "machine." The caterpillar thus gives form to
the uncreative imagination, and crushing the insect is the last act
possible to a state of mind that, having negated everything else, now
turns negatively against the image of itself. Its "last drop of poison"
spent in symbolic self-destruction, imagination is reborn as a creative
and visionary power, an emblem or prototype of the new heaven and
earth it foresees.

Violence, mystical vision, the nature of imagination—these are
familiar themes in Brontë's other literature, and "The Butterfly" has
been discussed as a foreshadowing of *Wuthering Heights.*[9] But the essays
also reveal aspects of Brontë's thinking that we otherwise rarely see. The
most pronounced of these is an attitude that can only be called cynical: a
view of human nature as inherently corrupt. Except for the heroic
Harold, the essays present mankind as mean, hypocritical, narrowly
self-interested. In "Filial Love" (*Essays in French,* pp. 13–14), Brontë
says that man's baseness is revealed in the fact that God has had to
command us to honor our parents: ". . . for human beings to perform
the tenderest and holiest of all duties, a threat is necessary." In the
commandment "is hidden a reproach bitterer than any open accusation
could express; a charge of total blindness or of infernal ingratitude."
Children wound and even kill their parents by their neglect and failure
to love. But in another essay, entitled "Lettre," the roles are reversed. A

lonely and neglected girl writes to her mother from school. She is in poor health, and, not having heard from her mother in a long time, is afraid that her mother is forgetting her. Although she utters no reproach, her letter is a desperate plea for a sign of parental love.[10] Even the closest family ties, as we saw in "A Letter from One Brother to Another," do not necessarily release warmth and affection.

Indeed, as Brontë describes the human race in "The Cat" (*Essays in French,* pp. 9–10), humans possess only negative qualities. A dog is infinitely too good for mankind to be compared to it, whereas the cat "is extremely like us in disposition." People and cats share the traits of hypocrisy, cruelty, and ingratitude—qualities that we call by their true name and condemn in cats, but call by another name and reward in ourselves. Thus a cat, to get something from its master, hides its true feeling and approaches him in a caressing, gentle manner, "rubs his pretty little head against him and sticks out his paw with a touch as soft as down." Its end obtained, the cat resumes its aloof, indifferent character. "Such finesse in him we call hypocrisy," Brontë says, "but in ourselves we give it another name politeness, and any person not using it to disguise his true feelings would soon be driven from society." Similarly, a fox-hunter torments his prey as ruthlessly as any cat; and for the "image, the true copy," of a darling child with a crushed butterfly "between his cruel little fingers," Brontë wishes she had a cat "with the half-swallowed tail of a rat hanging from his mouth." Finally, a cat's ingratitude is only "another name for shrewdness." Civilized society does not remove the viciousness that man shares with cats; it uses a form of double speak to justify it. Dropping the cynical attitude and diminishing the satirical tone, Brontë would explore the socially approved forms of violence further in *Wuthering Heights.*

"The Cat" is the first of the essays in French. The last and longest is an allegory entitled "The Palace of Death."[11] More formal and more strictly narrative than the other essays, it is also the most moralistic and fatalistic.

The narrative concerns Death's need for a prime minister—there are too many victims for old age to do the work alone. Assembled in the palace of Death to contend for the position are such human vices and natural evils as anger and vengeance, envy and treason, famine and plague; but the strongest candidates are ambition and fanaticism. The most skillful of the others, ambition says, can only trap a victim here

and there, and only those who are morally or physically weak. Ambition will bring Death the elite of mankind, those who were farthest
from Death's power and in their prime. Fanaticism argues that it has all
the power ambition boasts of and more. It can divide families and set
the son in opposition to his father, the daughter to her mother; it can
turn close friends into mortal enemies, and make the wife betray her
husband, the servant her master. Since the prime minister of Death
should be someone who is always close to men and in control of them,
the choice is between ambition and fanaticism—the deadliest and most
universal evils.

As Death wavers between the two, the doors of the room open and a
radiant, joyful person appears, light as the wind. This is intemperance,
and it is the most qualified to serve Death because only it can flourish
with the spread of civilization. As man becomes more civilized, he will
overcome ambition and fanaticism, will eradicate famine; but as civilization grows so will intemperance. It can infect the son through the
father, and before men unite to banish it from their society, it will have
changed their natures and made the entire species an easy prey for
Death, whose palace will be gorged with victims. Death is convinced.
All of the others can serve her as ministers, but to intemperance alone is
reserved the honor of being Death's viceroy.

The tone of the essay suggests that it was written in deadly earnest;
and although we cannot conclude from the essay alone that Brontë was a
Puritan, neither can we overlook the strongly puritanical view in the
only moral treatise of Brontë's that we have. Among the Gondalans, to
be sure, excessive and reckless pursuit of pleasure leads to ruin, and
Julius's judge warns him in prison,

> "Those who follow earthly pleasure,
> Heavenly knowledge will not lead;
> Wisdom hides from them her treasure,
> Virtue bids them evil-speed!"[12]

But our sympathies are probably more with Julius than his judge.
Brontë's characteristic position is to refrain from moral judgment
against her characters, or to balance one moral outlook against another:
to be open-minded or detached rather than rigid and condemnatory.
Emily was not seriously influenced by the austere views of her aunt,

although they lived in the same house for twenty years, and Miss Branwell did have an effect on Anne's religious outlook. Even when all this is granted, however, "The Palace of Death" remains an indictment of the human race worthy of the sternest Victorian moralist—or a Jonathan Swift.

Collectively, the essays image man to be deeply, if not irredeemably, flawed. The only instances of moral victory or salvation depend on extreme circumstances: the battle positions facing Harold, apocalypse in "The Butterfly," the brother's revulsion against his instinct for violence. Even these scenes are dominated by rivalry and struggle, the senseless machinations of man against man, life against life. The personified vices that debate in the palace of death divide and possess the human soul without opposition from any of the virtues; and though intemperance may seem an unusual vice for Brontë to choose as the chief—instead of, say, an intense Heathcliffian revenge or Gondalan ambition—her meaning is unmistakable and dark. The seeds of our spiritual destruction cannot be totally eradicated. The higher we rise on the civilized scale, the more certainly will we be doomed—the more subtly will we act like cats.[13] With nature existing on the principle of destruction, the human soul imaged as a parliament of sins, and society built upon disguise, the essays show us what Thomas Hardy was to call "a full look at the Worst."

Of course we have the visionary poems and *Wuthering Heights* to remind us that Brontë saw past the worst to the better, and that the vision of evil in the essays, like the image of the prison in the poems, is part of a larger, liberating imaginative scheme. There is the question, too, of how much weight should be placed on what were, after all, classroom exercises, based to some degree on the prose models Héger had the Brontës analyze. The Emily who wrote under direction at Brussels and the Emily who wrote what she wanted to write at home are not entirely one and the same writer. The cynicism of "The Cat" and "Filial Love," the desperate loneliness of "Lettre," the pervading sense of corruption and violence—these no doubt are attributable to Brontë's homesickness and isolation while preparing herself in a foreign land for a career she did not wholeheartedly desire. Working under the bitterest conditions her nature could endure, she wrote bitterly.

Emily Brontë was not a bitter person or a cynic, yet the essays cannot be dismissed as an isolated phase of her life or relegated to an unimpor-

tant corner of her imagination. They are the clearest indication we have
of how she saw the world before she reconstructed it in her poetry and
Wuthering Heights; and—at the same time—they show how habitual it
was for her, even in a classroom exercise, to express herself through
impersonation, irony, dramatic conflict and incident, the devices that
she used in her poems and her novel to detach herself from and
encompass and make vivid a violent world. Although the essays fall
considerably short of her major writings, Héger's method apparently
did not imperil her originality. The experience of writing the essays, in
fact, was a new one for her, and has an importance we can only
imperfectly estimate. For the first time Brontë was writing for a public
audience, a reader who would criticize and correct her, rather than for
her favorite sister. Surprisingly—when we consider how she would
object to Charlotte's discovery of her poems—Brontë rose to the
occasion, did not shrink back or compromise her thoughts because a
stranger would see them, and, whatever Héger's impression may have
been on her, she made a strong one on him. Writing in a foreign
language, perhaps she did not realize how self-revealing the essays
were, but there is no evidence that she thought of them merely as
exercises, once she began them, or that she wrote them to please another
or for any reason but to be true to herself. The essays contain the raw
material of Brontë's mature vision. Human nature appears in them
mostly in its unredeemed state, before it has been subjected to the
transforming power of imagination. When Brontë returned to this
material in *Wuthering Heights,* her next and last work written for the
public, her imagination recreated it and discovered the possibilities of
man's redemption.

Chapter Five

Wuthering Heights: Finding the Uses of Creation

"This is a strange book," wrote an early reviewer of *Wuthering Heights.* "It is not without evidences of considerable power: but, as a whole, it is wild, confused, disjointed, and improbable; and the people who make up the drama, which is tragic enough in its consequences, are savages ruder than those who lived before the days of Homer."[1] Today, although *Wuthering Heights* is generally acclaimed as a masterpiece, popular with both the ordinary reader and the professional scholar, it retains much of its strangeness. For May Sinclair, "There is no name for it. It is above all our consecrated labels and distinctions."[2] Dorothy Van Ghent calls it, "of all English novels, the most treacherous for the analytical understanding to approach."[3] Of the major Victorian novels, it is the most difficult to reduce to, or explain by, the conventions of its time. Is Heathcliff a hero larger than life, or a villain ruder than the savages who lived before Homer? Is Nelly Dean's point of view transparent, so that we see the characters objectively, or a distortion that twists them into the only shapes she can recognize? What is the meaning of Catherine Earnshaw's declaration that she is Heathcliff?[4]

We have learned that *Wuthering Heights,* far from being confused and disjointed, is beautifully orchestrated and planned, but such fundamental questions about it persist, and the book attracts the reader precisely because it gives no easy answers. The words most often applied to *Wuthering Heights* are those like "unique" and "original," as though this novel stood in a category or class by itself, a genre of one—yet, to adopt Blake's definition of vision, recognizably massive in its representation of what eternally exists.

Like Brontë's poetry, *Wuthering Heights* anticipates twentieth-century literature—in its complex point of view, its violence, its use of dramatic scene instead of authorial comment or summary, its moral impartiality. It transcends its time as few other Victorian novels do, yet it has points of connection with them and with the literary traditions of the nineteenth century. Emily Brontë was a Romantic in her quest for the unified self and totality of being; and she expresses just as strongly the Victorian crisis of the divided self and the resultant conflict between natural and social values. Like most major novelists from Dickens to Hardy, she was drawn to the figure of the orphan, and drew a composite orphan-symbol in Heathcliff and Hareton. She uses, in fact, a number of familiar literary conventions or themes. *Wuthering Heights* is a revenge story, in which Heathcliff, like the illegitimate Edmund in *King Lear,* plots to dispossess Hindley of the Heights, and almost brings havoc to all the Earnshaws and Lintons. Brontë read Gothic fiction, and her description of the Heights resembles that of typical Gothic mansions—mysterious, isolated dwellings, with dark passages and locked rooms, where one encounters ghostly horrors and the super-natural. Heathcliff's ancestry includes the Byronic hero and possibly Milton's Satan. Like them, Heathcliff is a dark, morose, violent man tormented by his fierce desire and his loss. Stories of an ill-fated love, in which one of the lovers dies and returns from the grave to haunt the other, occur in ballad and folk tale.[5] There are some specific parallels to *Wuthering Heights* in "The Bridegroom of Barna," a story which appeared in 1840, in *Blackwood's Magazine.* In "The Bridegroom of Barna," set in a remote district of Ireland, an outlaw, Hugh Lawlor, visits the grave of his bride, digs up her corpse, and holds it in his arms, as Heathcliff holds the dead body of Catherine.[6]

But whatever Brontë may have recalled or used from her readings, *Wuthering Heights* is not a conventional or formula novel. It is the cosmic vision of an imagination that for years had turned mostly to its own symbols and myths and expressed itself in secret poems. And it is not so much the portrait of a given society, as an exposure of the principles of social existence—an epic comedy, despite its violence, that moves from a state of division and war to union and peace. If *Wuthering Heights* is unique, it is not because Brontë did not share the concerns of other Victorians, but because she dealt with what was timeless and universal in them, and because her intensity and thoroughness took her past the limits her contemporaries had learned to accept.[7]

The Plot

The chronology of *Wuthering Heights* is somewhat complex. The story begins in 1801, and is written as a journal account by Mr. Lockwood, a Londoner who has rented Thrushcross Grange and who, in November of that year, visits his landlord, Heathcliff, at the Heights. Most of the story takes place in the late eighteenth century, however, and Lockwood hears it from Nelly Dean, his housekeeper, who has lived at the Heights or the Grange all of her life. Lockwood leaves the area in January 1802 and does not return until September, when Nelly tells him what has happened during his absence. Brontë's narrative method keeps the reader always at one and usually at two removes from the central characters of the story. When a character like Isabella Linton describes events to Nelly who then describes them to Lockwood, the reader is thrice removed.

Wuthering Heights, an isolated dwelling in wild moor land, is the ancestral home of the Earnshaw family; Thrushcross Grange, its nearest neighbor and home of the Linton family, is three miles away. Returning from a trip to Liverpool, Mr. Earnshaw brings with him a dark child he found in the streets, and whom the family names Heathcliff. Hindley, the older of the two Earnshaw children, hates Heathcliff because of his father's partiality for him, but his sister Catherine attaches herself to Heathcliff, and he to her, until the two are close, inseparable friends. After the death of Mr. Earnshaw, Hindley returns from school with a wife, and treating Heathcliff as a servant, abuses and degrades him. Heathcliff and Catherine solace each other and roam the moors, until on an excursion to Thrushcross Grange Catherine is bitten on the ankle by the Linton's dog. Forced to remain at the Grange for six weeks, Catherine learns a different and more gentle set of manners, and returns to the Heights an elegant young lady instead of the tomboy she had been. Next to Edgar Linton, who begins to court Catherine, Heathcliff seems ruder and more savage than ever. Although she knows that her soul and Heathcliff's are the same, Catherine feels she could never marry him—they would be penniless. And on hearing her say that it would degrade her to marry him, Heathcliff disappears from the Heights.

He does not return for three years. In the meantime, Catherine has survived a serious illness and is married to Edgar Linton. Heathcliff's reappearance awakens her old attachment to him, however, and Heathcliff's love for her has never abated. Somehow Heathcliff has acquired the outward refinements of a gentleman, but his inner self is unchanged, and he begins a systematic revenge against Hindley and the Lintons. Living at the Heights, he encourages Hindley's drinking, gambles with him until he owns most of Hindley's property, and steals the affection of Hindley's son Hareton, whom he plans to degrade as Hindley had degraded him. Heathcliff's visits to the Grange provoke a crisis—Edgar is jealous of him as a rival and then alarmed that his sister Isabella has fallen in love with Heathcliff. After a violent scene between the two men, Catherine falls seriously ill again, and Heathcliff and Isabella elope.

Catherine never fully recovers, but dies giving birth to her daughter, Catherine Linton. Shortly afterwards, Isabella escapes from the tormenting atmosphere of the Heights to live in London, where she gives birth to Heathcliff's son, Linton Heathcliff. Hindley dies, and Heathcliff is master of the Heights. Yet he lives in torment because of the loss of Catherine, and waits to avenge himself against Edgar, the man who took her from him.

Twelve years pass without any communication between the houses, and Cathy Linton is thirteen before she discovers the existence of the Heights and her cousin Hareton, whose ignorance offends her. After Isabella's death, Linton Heathcliff, a peevish, sickly child, is brought to the Grange, but immediately claimed by his father. Heathcliff wants to possess Thrushcross Grange, which his son will inherit from Edgar, and he wants Linton to marry Cathy, which would give Heathcliff control over her and her personal property as well. His efforts succeed. Edgar is too ill to interfere, and though Linton Heathcliff is in no better health a romance develops between him and Cathy through love letters and secret visits to the Heights. At last, Heathcliff imprisons Cathy at the Heights until she consents to marry Linton. They do marry, but Cathy is able to break out of the Heights in time to see her father before he dies.

Linton Heathcliff dies shortly afterwards, and Heathcliff is master of both houses with seemingly absolute power over their two representatives, Hareton and Cathy. At first, there is only friction between the cousins, as Cathy rebukes Hareton's attempts to improve his mind and become friends with her. But her loneliness oppresses her, and she begins to desire Hareton's companionship. The enemies become allies and lovers—Hareton's native intelligence shows itself despite his coarse upbringing. Strangely, Heathcliff does not oppose them. Although he has the power to destroy both houses, he has lost the will to destroy. He becomes moody and abstract and cannot eat; he says that Catherine's spirit is visible to him. After four days of fasting, Heathcliff is found dead in Catherine's old bed. There are rumors that his ghost and Catherine's walk the moors, but this does not trouble Hareton and Cathy, who on New Year's Day will be married and move to the Grange. The Heights will be shut up and left to the care of the old servant, Joseph.

The following is a genealogical chart of the two principal families in *Wuthering Heights*. Catherine Linton, the married name of Catherine Earnshaw, is also the name of her daughter. To avoid confusion, I will refer to the mother as Catherine and the daughter as Cathy. The dates of the birth and death of the characters are those given by Charles Percy Sanger.[8]

Mr. and Mrs. Earnshaw				Mr. and Mrs. Linton	
Hindley x Frances		Catherine x Edgar		Heathcliff x Isabella	
(1757–	(d. 1778)	(1765–	(1762–	(1764–	(1765–
1784)		1784)	1801)	1802)	1797)
Hareton		Cathy		Linton	
(b. 1778)		(b. 1784)		(1784–1801)	

The Divided World of *Wuthering Heights*

Wuthering Heights portrays the universe in microcosm, and it is a massive, epical book, although by Victorian standards it is short and extremely compact. There are barely a dozen characters in it. Its entire world is framed by the Heights at one edge and the Grange at the other. Yet the two houses and their families represent and unleash fundamental forces of life. Together they give a total symbol of existence, while in their conflict they divide existence. This division produces a profound dualism, different scales of value, different notions of the ingredients of identity. We see an instance of this duality when Cathy Linton tells

Nelly of an argument with Linton Heathcliff about how best to spend a summer day.

> He said the pleasantest manner of spending a hot July day was lying from morning till evening on a bank of heath in the middle of the moors, with the bees humming dreamily about among the bloom, and the larks singing high up over head, and the blue sky and bright sun shining steadily and cloudlessly. That was his most perfect idea of heaven's happiness. Mine was rocking in a rustling green tree, with a west wind blowing, and bright, white clouds flitting rapidly above; and not only larks, but throstles, and blackbirds, and linnets, and cuckoos pouring out music on every side, and the moors seen at a distance, broken into cool dusky dells; but close by, great swells of long grass undulating in waves to the breeze; and woods and sounding water, and the whole world awake and wild with joy. He wanted all to lie in an ecstacy of peace; I wanted all to sparkle, and dance in a glorious jubilee.
>
> I said his heaven would be only half alive, and he said mine would be drunk; I said I should fall asleep in his, and he said he could not breathe in mine, and began to grow very snappish. (ch. 24, pp. 198–99)[9]

The issue goes beyond the question of enjoying a summer day to become a definition of heaven: the two have different visions of life at its most intense or perfect. Linton, the boy, identifies with traditionally female qualities of passivity and quiescence, whereas Cathy identifies with traditionally male qualities of activity and exertion.

Neither Cathy nor Linton goes as far as their respective parents, Catherine Earnshaw and Heathcliff, who reject the heaven of traditional Christianity for one which only they can identify and share. Catherine and Heathcliff belong to the Earnshaws and the Heights, whereas Cathy and Linton have been brought up as Lintons, and despite their argument, their division is smaller than that between the Earnshaws and the Lintons, the Heights and the Grange. The two houses split the whole of existence into opposite spheres that contend for mastery over the whole—either by refusing to recognize the reality of its opposite or by clashing against it. Unconscious, intensely subjective desires versus conscious, public standards; passion versus reason; energy versus restraint; the lawless and the law-abiding—it is such contraries as these, opposite and interdependent as darkness and light, that Emily Brontë evokes in the drama between the Earnshaws and the Lintons.[10]

The Heights is outside the law, outside the codes and forms of restraint imposed by society and civilized values—at least after the introduction of Heathcliff, whom we can consider as an Earnshaw. The Earnshaws have no limit to their passions, but love and hate with equal intensity, as if gripped by a monomania that will not allow compromise, that cannot heed the voice of reason or even of self-preservation. Hindley's torment after the death of his wife, Frances, is as extreme and obliterating of all else as is Heathcliff's after the death of Catherine. And it is as savage, as the early reviewer was correct to point out. *Wuthering Heights* is a violent novel; the Heights is the home or incarnation of violence. At one point Hindley pushes a knife between Nelly's teeth. Hareton hangs a litter of puppies by a chair-back. Heathcliff kidnaps Cathy Linton and Nelly and imprisons them at the Heights. He tortures and beats his son into submission to his will, and when he no longers needs him, he indifferently lets Linton Heathcliff die. Catherine is wild and unrelenting and given to paroxysms of emotion that lead to her self-destruction. Between Heathcliff and Hindley there exists an unremitting, brutal state of war, and on the night of Catherine's funeral, the two enact a particularly savage scene. Hindley has locked the Heights and waits for Heathcliff with a pistol that has a switch-blade knife in its barrel. He has vowed to kill him if Heathcliff attempts to enter the house. Heathcliff bursts open a window, and as the gun goes off the knife stabs into Hindley's wrist, causing him to faint. Heathcliff then grinds Hindley's head against the stones of the fireplace.

The Heights releases those forces that cannot be civilized, or that resist civilization—forces that spring from an almost obsessive will to power. As its opposite, Thrushcross Grange is a place of order, of submission to the rule of social law and convention. Life at the Grange is kept within bounds, just as the Grange—unlike the wild, exposed landscape of the Heights—exists as a well-planned park within the boundary of its walls. A pack of half-wild dogs prowls the recesses and dark corners of the Heights; at the Grange we find a library with rows of books. Old Mr. Linton and Edgar after him are magistrates or guardians of the law, and the Grange itself is subject to elaborate procedures of the law as enacted in Mr. Linton's will—whereas control of the Heights is a contest of power and chance between Heathcliff and Hindley. During her convalescence at the Grange, Catherine acquires a new and refined appearance and manners; it is her initiation from her original state of nature into society. Lockwood, the Londoner, used to the conventions and formal rules of society, has little difficulty adapting to life at the Grange; with its very different rules, the Heights is alien and threatening to him. Anything is possible at the Heights. There is a moral code and public sense of right and wrong at the Grange.

The contrast between the two houses and families, between the self-willed violators of the law and the socially conscious guardians of the law, informs the entire narrative and is the structural principle of Brontë's vision. What is perceived as real, or as necessary to existence, she shows, changes from one house to the other, from the value system supplied only by the self to that of a community or a tradition. Both Hindley and Edgar lose their wives early in marriage, for instance, and react so differently as to cause Nelly to compare their moral characters.

> I used to . . . perplex myself to explain satisfactorily why their conduct was so opposite in similar circumstances. They had both been fond husbands, and were both attached to their children; and I could not see how they shouldn't both have taken the same road, for good or evil. But, I thought in my mind, Hindley, with apparently the stronger head, has shown himself sadly the worse and the weaker man. When his ship struck, the captain abandoned his post; and the crew, instead of trying to save her, rushed into riot and confusion, leaving no hope for their luckless vessel. Linton, on the contrary, displayed the true courage of a loyal and faithful soul: he trusted God; and God comforted him. One hoped, and the other despaired: they chose their own lots, and were righteously doomed to endure them. (ch. 17, p. 152)

Edgar's personal tragedy does not shake his belief in a morally ordered universe or his trust in God. He controls his grief and lives afterwards as regularly and methodically as before. Hindley rages against God; Frances's death deprives him of his reasoning power—Nelly's metaphorical captain—and it makes the universe irrational and purposeless. Edgar, practicing traditional Christianity, can find comfort in his loss by submission to an absolute being that exists independently of himself. Hindley's loss is absolute: the self has no recourse or refuge in the void the loss has left. One can still seek for meaning in life; the other sees only meaninglessness.

Nelly's attitudes here—her approval of Edgar's way, her criticism of or inability to understand Hindley's—identify her as an ally of the Lintons and an adherent to the values embodied in the Grange. She measures Hindley by the Linton standard and finds him lacking. This is typical of the way each house views the other, and their limited perceptions of each other can be just as destructive as the physical conflicts which the perceptions result in. Approving of different values, following different schemes of moral sanction, each house makes the other the devil in its scheme—its enemy or symbol of evil. Each scheme is the other in reverse, so that the good of one house is the evil of the other, and the same event leads Edgar to hope and Hindley to despair. Catherine Earnshaw trades the freedom of the Heights for the restraint of the Grange, and becomes an exile; Isabella Linton trades the order of the Grange for the anarchy of the Heights, and becomes an exile. Each house and its conditions appear in radically different terms, depending on whether one's perspective has been shaped by the values of that house or by those of the other. The Grange is Catherine's prison, as the Heights is Isabella's.[11]

We saw Brontë using point of view in the Gondal poems to create composite portraits of characters like Augusta Almeda and Julius. Augusta's image of herself differs from her image for others, so that her identity changes according to the position from which we see her. In *Wuthering Heights,* there is an almost impenetrable barrier between the self-identity of each house and its identity for the other, and when one family uses its standards to perceive and measure the other, it does violence to the other. Heathcliff cannot be judged by the rules that prevail at the Grange, yet that is precisely what the Lintons do. His complexion is too dark, his manners too abrupt, for Heathcliff to appear to the Lintons as anything other than rude and boorish—a threat to their cherished values. At their first meeting, when Heathcliff is a boy, old Mr. Linton pronounces him a criminal, and suggests—perhaps half mockingly—that he should be hung at once, before his criminality emerges (ch. 6, p. 49). Hareton appears as a dunce to Cathy, who disowns her cousinship with him. Someone who cannot restrict her self-expression to the forms of behavior her society approves of, like Catherine, must appear selfish, wild, and abandoned next to an Edgar Linton, which is the picture of Catherine consistently drawn by Nelly.

Catherine and Heathcliff's insistence on a self that is bound only by its own rules can only seem destructive to the Lintons, who live by the social contract and the necessity for compromise and restraint. On the same basis, social compromise and restraint can only seem destructive to the Earnshaws, for whom the self is absolute. And in fact the Earnshaws make the same mistake as the Lintons, by judging the ways of the Grange according to what is valued at the Heights. Heathcliff scoffs at the idea that Edgar loves Catherine, because Edgar does not love in the only way Heathcliff can recognize: "If he loved with all the powers of his puny being, he couldn't love as much in eighty years as I could in a day" (ch. 14, p. 126). He goes on to denounce his wife, Isabella, as a "pitiful, slavish, mean-minded brach." In an early scene, Hindley tells Edgar, after Heathcliff has thrown a dish of hot apple-sauce in his face, to "take the law into your own fists—it will give you an appetite!" (ch. 7, p. 56). Later, Catherine locks Heathcliff and Edgar in the Grange kitchen and, throwing the key into the fire, tells her husband to fight it out with Heathcliff, a much stronger man than the frail Edgar.

The Lintons understand only degrees of conformity to the law; the Earnshaws understand only degrees of self-assertion. This division in the world of *Wuthering Heights* persists and intensifies until the final union between Cathy and Hareton. Neither side has insight into the conditions of the other—Nelly, who understands and values only what is apparent to common sense, cannot see that Hindley is an alcoholic and compulsive neurotic: to her, he simply chose his lot. When Heathcliff tells her that he has done no injustice or anything else to repent of, and that he is in sight of his heaven, Nelly cannot comprehend him. She does not even attempt to understand Catherine's declaration, "I am Heathcliff," the meaning of which is incommunicable except to Catherine and Heathcliff. Neither side makes a genuine attempt to remove the barriers blocking communication. Linton Heathcliff mocks Hareton's Yorkshire accent. Heathcliff keeps the Heights locked and closed. Edgar forbids Cathy to go beyond the walls enclosing the Grange land.

Yet Cathy does pass the walls and is drawn to the Heights. Emily Brontë has divided the world into opposites that conflict with and antagonize each other, yet are attracted to each other: Isabella to

Heathcliff, Heathcliff to the gentlemanly appearance of an Edgar Linton, Edgar and Catherine to each other, Hindley to Frances, an outsider with the social values of the Lintons. The attraction to an opposite identity suggests a potential in each for precisely that which is felt to be most foreign or alien to the self each is conscious of—or for what has been denied and forbidden them by the Heights or the Grange: social equality for Heathcliff, reckless adventure for Isabella. Her attraction to Heathcliff, of course, is shortlived, and he uses her only to further his plot against Edgar. But Isabella changes at the Heights, as a latent Earnshaw principle in her begins to emerge. Hindley shows her the gun with the knife attached to its barrel, and as Isabella describes the scene to Nelly, it is clear that her reaction surprises and even shocks her. "I surveyed the weapon inquisitively; a hideous notion struck me. How powerful I should be possessing such an instrument! I took it from his hand, and touched the blade. He looked astonished at the expression my face assumed during a brief second. It was not horror, it was covetousness" (ch. 13, p. 119). A Freudian would almost certainly interpret the pistol as a sexual or phallic symbol; but we need not identify it as such to see that traits of her personality that Isabella suppressed at the Grange are coming to the surface at the Heights. It was her suppressed, secret self that was attracted to Heathcliff. In this and a number of other scenes, Brontë suggests that the two houses, although divided and opposed in their perceptions of each other, have an underlying unity. If in nothing else, they are the same in their violence. A more peaceful and positive union is possible only after an Earnshaw has accepted the Linton principle in him, and a Linton the Earnshaw in her, and the violence has been spent.

In the power struggles and extreme passions of the Earnshaws, we see violence incarnate and unrestrained. When Heathcliff threatens to tell Mr. Earnshaw that Hindley has thrashed him, unless Hindley trades horses with him, Hindley hits Heathcliff in the breast with an iron weight (ch. 4, p. 41). When Lockwood steps into the Heights for the first time, he is attacked by a pack of dogs. Violence, reliance on power, is the acknowledged rule of the Heights. At the Grange, violence is concealed and given acceptable forms. Yet the capacity for raw violence is present, as in Isabella's coveting the gun. When Catherine locks Edgar and Heathcliff in the Grange kitchen, and Edgar has, literally, his back to the wall, he strikes Heathcliff in the throat with "a blow that would have levelled a slighter man" (ch. 11, p. 100). Then Edgar relies on his retainers, each armed with a bludgeon. When Heathcliff and Catherine first visit the Grange and look through the drawing room window, the sight seems beautiful to them. "We should have thought ourselves in heaven," Heathcliff says (ch. 6, p. 47). But Isabella is screaming at one end of the room, and Edgar is weeping. Between them is their pet dog, which they have nearly pulled in two in their quarrel. Hearing laughter outside the window, the young Lintons run to their parents who let loose a bulldog, which catches Catherine by the ankle. It is when the two vagabonds are brought into the house that Mr. Linton, a magistrate, says of Heathcliff, "the villain scowls so plainly in his face, would it not be a kindness to the country to hang him at once, before he shows his nature in acts, as well as features" (ch. 6, p. 49). The law relies upon violence to protect itself against those who are—or look—outside the law. Later, we discover that one of the dogs prowling the floors of the Heights is an offspring of the dog that attacked Catherine at the Grange (ch. 13, p. 122).

One of the most violent scenes in the novel, although it occurs at the Heights, belongs to Lockwood, the tenant of the Grange. Lockwood's nightmare of Catherine's ghost is also one of the most controversial and unforgettable incidents in *Wuthering Heights,* shocking when it comes and yet prepared for in a way that shows Brontë's art at its finest.

Lockwood is the narrator; in the opening chapters, of course, he is as unaware of the history of the Heights as is the reader, who tends to identify with Lockwood—an outsider, an ordinary man who has internalized the conventions of his world. He visits the Heights fully expecting his conventions to operate there as in London. Also, he wants his tea; he thinks it dangerously possible that Cathy will become too interested in him; he thinks that he and Heathcliff are men of similar character—overly reserved and averse to showy display of feeling. None of his assumptions proves true, his conventions are ignored, and he does not find any of the values at the Heights that he thought he would. In effect, he has crossed the threshold into a very different world from the society he has known—an elemental, violent state in which his first experience is the attack of the dogs. Although he does not identify or seem to profit by it as such, Lockwood is undergoing a process of initiation in which the first truth he learns is that outside of the law, past the social limits, exists a state of fierce antagonisms.

But in terms of Brontë's symbolism, on the other side of the social limits is the unconsciousness: the outlawed self held in check by the social consciousness. And on his second visit to the Heights, Lockwood crosses the threshold into this unconsciousness and learns the further truth that violence is in him—a representative of the law by day, a violent man in his dreams. Given the bed that used to be Catherine's, Lockwood has two dreams. In the first, Lockwood dreams he has gone to Gimmerden Chapel to hear a discourse on sin, "Seventy Times Seven, and the First of the Seventy-First," divided into 490 parts, each equal to an ordinary sermon. The sins, Lockwood says, "were of the most curious character—odd transgressions that I never imagined previously" (ch. 3, p. 29). When the preacher, Jabes Branderham, reaches the first of the seventy-first, the unforgivable sin, Lockwood accuses him of having committed it in his interminable address on the first 490. Branderham, in turn, accuses Lockwood for his ill reception of the sermon, and exhorts the congregation, all armed with staves, to attack him. In the violence that follows, "the whole chapel resounded with rappings and counter-rappings. Every man's hand was against his neighbor; and Branderham, unwilling to remain idle, poured forth his zeal in a shower of loud taps on the boards of the pulpit . . ." (ch. 3, p. 29). The dogs of the early scene have become the people in this, and can now be seen as symbolic of the violence that lies concealed in man and his institutions.

The Chapel scene is a definite dream, from which Lockwood is wakened by the supposed rappings of Branderham to discover the source of the sound in the branch of a fir tree against his window. Then Lockwood dreams again—only now the line between conscious and unconscious states is more ambiguous, and apparently he is in a half-sleep. Lockwood knows that he is in Catherine's bed, and still hears the branch rubbing against his window. To stop the noise, he has to break the glass and reach out for the branch. Instead of the branch, his fingers "closed on the fingers of a little, ice-cold hand":

> The intense horror of nightmare came over me; I tried to draw back my arm, but the hand clung to it, and a most melancholy voice sobbed—
>
> "Let me in—let me in!"
>
> "Who are you?" I asked, struggling, meanwhile, to disengage myself.
>
> "Catherine Linton," it replied, shiveringly. . . . "I'm come home, I'd lost my way on the moor!"

As it spoke, I discerned, obscurely, a child's face looking through the window. Terror made me cruel; and, finding it useless to attempt shaking the creature off, I pulled its wrist on to the broken pane, and rubbed it to and fro till the blood ran down and soaked the bed-clothes: still it wailed, "Let me in!" and maintained its tenacious gripe, almost maddening me with fear. (ch. 3, p. 30)

Terror, Lockwood says, made him cruel; and it causes him to act as savagely as Heathcliff does, when fear or despair or hatred makes Heathcliff cruel.[12]

Lockwood, the civilized man, has become one with Heathcliff. The civilized man suppresses his capacity for violence so that it goes underground to emerge in dreams; or he organizes violence into capital punishment. But civilization does not transcend or eliminate its underlying violence—a lesson from history which Emily had already incorporated into the Gondal myth. Lockwood is somewhat foppish, his supposed misanthropy a mere shadow of Heathcliff's, and his summer flirtation with a "fascinating creature" a parody of Heathcliff and Catherine. Yet his dream—the return of Catherine—fulfills Heathcliff's deepest desire: Lockwood's dream is Heathcliff's dream. When Lockwood is unconscious, when the guardian of his mind and its social code is asleep, he becomes a Heathcliff, just as Edgar does when he strikes Heathcliff in the throat. The intimation of that, no less than the face of the ghost, must terrify Lockwood; afterwards, when he is awake and fully conscious, he dismisses the dream as the "persecutions" of Heathcliff's ancestors (ch. 3, p. 31). In the next chapter, the novel begins to trace the past, and to move from Lockwood's involuntary assumption of Heathcliff's role to Catherine's emphatic assertion that she is Heathcliff.

The Divided Self in *Wuthering Heights*

Catherine says, simply and enigmatically, "I am Heathcliff" (ch. 9, p. 74). Yet she has just been telling Nelly why she has chosen to take on another identity and be Mrs. Edgar Linton, mistress of Thrushcross Grange. More than any other character, Catherine internalizes the divisions of *Wuthering Heights.* Even as a girl, in her early teens, she has acquired different identities, symbolized by the names that Lockwood reads on her window ledge: Catherine Earnshaw, Catherine Heathcliff, Catherine Linton. If Catherine Earnshaw is Catherine Heathcliff, she is also Catherine Linton. The two men whose names she takes on awaken her to different possibilities or necessities of being, satisfy different needs, and create incompatible selves in her which she cannot reconcile or transcend except in death.

But Catherine's attachment to Heathcliff is so intense, so like a contact with an elemental life force, that her decision to marry Edgar seems—and possibly is—a tragic mistake, a denial of her essential self for a more superficial identity based on class standing and social status.[13] Catherine herself speaks of her love for Heathcliff as the eternal foundation underneath her life with Edgar; time will never change it, whereas her love for Edgar is like "the foliage in the woods," and will change as the trees change in winter (ch. 9, p. 74). Catherine feels that by marrying Edgar she is betraying her soul, the vital principle that she and Heathcliff have in common. "Whatever our souls are made of," she says, "his and mine are the same, and Linton's is as different as a moonbeam from lightning, or frost from fire" (ch. 9, p. 72). Later, just before she dies, Heathcliff accuses her of leaving him for a "poor fancy" that she felt for Edgar: "Because misery, and degradation, and death, and nothing that God or Satan could inflict would have parted us, *you,* of your own will, did it" (ch. 15, p. 135).

Why, then, does she marry Edgar Linton when she is eternally one with Heathcliff, and when Heathcliff "comprehends in his person" her feelings to Edgar and herself? Nelly says it is because Catherine is selfish, "wicked," or else ignorant of the duties involved in marriage (ch. 9, p. 74)—a brutally inadequate response. If it is a tragic mistake to marry Edgar, no one can be more aware of it as such than Catherine, who feels the wrong in her soul. Yet marriage with Heathcliff is impossible: they would be penniless, and Catherine is right when she says, "It would degrade me to marry Heathcliff now" (ch. 9, p. 72). Catherine's own reasons for marrying Edgar are that he is handsome and pleasant to be with, young, cheerful, and rich; she will like being the greatest woman in the neighborhood, and she will be "proud of having such a husband" (ch. 9, p. 70). Catherine is not a materialist or an opportunist, but neither is she the primitive, wild girl who ran on the moors with Heathcliff. Her convalescence at the Grange changed and socialized her—made her aware of the identity that she has for and in her society. When she returns to the Heights, she has grown up in a way Heathcliff has not, and has been exposed to values that Heathcliff cannot share and to needs he cannot satisfy—they no longer converse. "Should I always be sitting with you?" Catherine asks him. "What good do I get? What do you talk about? You might be dumb or a baby for anything you say to amuse me, or for anything you do, either!" (ch. 8, p. 64). Before his disappearance and change, Heathcliff is duller than Edgar, who is Catherine's mental as well as social equal. Catherine and Edgar have much in common, and unless she is totally deluded or lying, she loves him: "I love all his looks, and all his actions, and him entirely, and altogether" (ch. 9, p. 71). Because her love for Heathcliff is necessary, it does not follow that her love for Edgar is not real.

Nor is her love for Edgar a poor fancy, as Heathcliff charges. But it depends on accidental rather than intrinsic qualities. Catherine would not love Edgar if he were ugly and poor. Her love for Edgar Linton, the identity of Catherine Linton, is necessary to her as a member of a community. Her love for Heathcliff is necessary in and of itself—and it is never presented as subject to her choice. Catherine is aware of the difference, as her comparisons make clear; and though she is attracted to Edgar's refined manners and appearance, she does not mistake appearance for reality, or lose sight of the existence which she calls eternal because she adapts to her place and time. She was wrong to think she could fuse the two together, but she never means to desert Heathcliff. Separation from him is out of the question for her. Heathcliff is her inviolable self, as intimate to her as her own self-consciousness; and he is the other-than-self that the self reaches towards, to become one with, and thus escape its own finite limits and discover the uses of creation. "I cannot express it," Catherine says to Nelly, "but surely you and everybody have a notion that there is, or should be, an existence of yours beyond you. What were the use of my creation if I were entirely contained here. My great miseries in this world have been Heathcliff's miseries, and I watched and felt each from the beginning; my great thought in living is himself. If all else perished, and *he* remained, I should still continue to be; and if all else remained, and he were annihilated, the Universe would turn to a mighty stranger. I should not seem a part of it" (ch. 9, pp. 73–74). Catherine's language has become religious: it identifies the indispensable factor of her existence. In these terms, though no one category encompasses Catherine's meaning, her faith resembles Brontë's in "No coward soul":

> Though Earth and moon were gone
> And suns and universes ceased to be
> And thou wert left alone
> Every Existence would exist in thee.
>   (*Complete Poems,* #191, p. 243)[14]

Nelly thinks Catherine is speaking "nonsense." Even to the sympathetic reader, her meaning is elusive. Brontë addresses herself to God—a universal concept. What Catherine is attempting to express through her relationship with Heathcliff, though it is as fundamental as a religion, is private: it is the self which no one who is not herself can know. When Catherine says, "I am Heathcliff," she joins her existence, her unique knowledge of what it means "to be," with his, so that the words are meaningful only to herself and Heathcliff. When Heathcliff does the same, and expresses his existence as only he can, for only he has lived it, he speaks in terms that only he and Catherine can understand. If he is the predicate or complement of her "I am," she is his soul and life: "Be with me always—take any form—drive me mad! only *do* not leave me in this abyss, where I cannot find you! Oh, God, it is unutterable! I *cannot* live without my life! I *cannot* live without my soul!" (ch. 16, p. 139). He is suffering the catastrophe that Catherine said would come to her should he perish and all else remain. It is unutterable, Heathcliff says; I can't express it, Catherine says. The self that they share, the experience of being two in one, is beyond language, outside the conventions and limits of speech, like the deep truth that Shelley said is imageless. The bond of their union, the origin of which is never explained, is that between them there is no barrier between knower and known, self and other, subject and object. In their mutual identity, such distinctions cease to have meaning, and communication of the self is both complete and unnecessary.[15]

Yet other barriers remain, and it is isolation, not union, that dominates the lives of the first generation. Their physical bodies separate Catherine and Heathcliff, and the self can be locked inside a given role or set of assumptions, which it is unaware of or compelled by. Catherine makes a fatal mistake in thinking that Heathcliff will accept her marriage for the good that she will then be able to do him—and in thinking that Edgar would agree to her plan. Heathcliff is willing to jeopardize Catherine's life to satisfy his need to see her, and his visit precipitates the final crisis which kills her. Edgar insists that she choose between them, and thus sacrifice one part of her being for the other: "Will you give up Heathcliff hereafter, or will you give up me? It is impossible for you to be *my* friend and *his* at the same time; and I absolutely *require* to know which you choose" (ch. 11, p. 102). Apparently, she cannot give up either: the very difference between the two men, the different selfhood and values they stand for, makes it impossible for either to replace the other. As Catherine becomes a battleground between the Heights and the Grange, she loses energy and life, and ultimately is unable to distinguish between the two houses. Speaking to Nelly at the Grange, she sees the black clothes-press of her old room at the Heights.

"The black press? where is that?" I asked. "You are talking in your sleep!"

"It's against the wall, as it always is," she replied. "It *does* appear odd—I see a face in it!"

"There is no press in the room, and never was," said I. . . .

"Don't *you* see that face?" she enquired, gazing earnestly at the mirror.

And say what I could, I was incapable of making her comprehend it to be her own; so I rose and covered it with a shawl.

"It's behind there still!" she pursued anxiously. "And it stirred. Who is it? I hope it will not come out when you are gone! Oh! Nelly, the room is haunted! I'm afraid of being alone!"

I took her hand in mine, and bid her be composed, for a succession of shudders convulsed her frame, and she *would* keep straining her gaze towards the glass.

"There's nobody here!" I insisted. "It was *yourself*, Mrs. Linton; you knew it a while since."

"Myself," she gasped, "and the clock is striking twelve! It's true, then; that's dreadful!" (ch. 12, pp. 105–106)

She thought she was lying in her bedroom at the Heights, but can no longer recognize herself as she was at the Heights, before her unity of being was broken, and she and Heathcliff were each other's all in all. Now, in what is a state of extreme inner division, the old self has become a stranger that haunts her.

"Why am I so changed?" Catherine asks. "I wish I were a girl again, half savage, and hardy, and free." It is as if the years since she was twelve

years old had vanished, and she had been "wrenched from the Heights
. . . and been converted at a stroke into Mrs. Linton" (ch. 12, p. 107).
Catherine is eighteen; she was fifteen when she accepted Edgar's pro-
posal, and seventeen when she married him. She has experienced, in a
particularly intense way, the loss of innocence, the adolescent sexual
crisis, that occurs throughout Victorian fiction. Heathcliff is
Catherine's companion in her presexual years; Edgar's entrance in her
life coincides with the advent of her adult sexuality, but although she
chooses him as her marriage partner, Edgar does not seem to arouse
strong sexual feelings in Catherine or to show them himself. Physical
desire for each other does not characterize their marriage, but appears
instead between Catherine and Heathcliff. It is those two, outside the
law, and not Catherine and her husband, that are the central focus of
Wuthering Heights, in so far as it is a love story. Moreover, Heathcliff
embodies the Victorian conception of male sexuality: dark, physically
imposing, imperious, and secret; Edgar satisfies the Victorian ideal of
the husband. Indeed, the split in Victorian literature between the
two—between the sexually active partner who is morally undesirable or
prohibited, and the sexually passive partner who is within the law and
acceptable—is so widespread that it is no surprise to find the same
division in *Wuthering Heights* (both types appear in *Jane Eyre*). Just as
Heathcliff makes Catherine aware of her unique being, and is necessary
to her being, so he makes her aware of her passions and satisfies her
strongest emotional needs. It is only with Heathcliff or, in her terms, as
Heathcliff, that Catherine can release her feelings as strongly as they
require to be released. When her feelings are released, then, that is
being Heathcliff. As a child, when her sexuality is latent, Catherine can
be uninhibited in the expression of her emotions and in her attachment
to Heathcliff. Later, as she becomes conscious of the sexual nature or
implications of her emotions, she can no longer be so free. At twelve—
that is, before adolescence—there is no division between what
Catherine feels and what she can express. At fifteen, she has acquired
sexual feelings and a public role that will not allow her to express them
except as the wife of Edgar Linton.

As Heathcliff is outside the law, the passions and especially the
sexual feelings he arouses are forbidden, and at once alien and indifferent to the social consciousness of Nelly, who describes the last, explo-
sive scene between Heathcliff and Catherine:

In her eagerness she rose and supported herself on the arm of the chair. At that earnest appeal, he turned to her, looking absolutely desperate. His eyes wide, and wet at last, flashed fiercely on her; his breast heaved convulsively. An instant they held asunder; and then how they met I hardly saw, but Catherine made a spring, and he caught her, and they were locked in an embrace from which I thought my mistress would never be released alive. In fact, to my eyes, she seemed directly insensible. He flung himself into the nearest seat, and on my approaching hurriedly to ascertain if she had fainted, he gnashed at me, and foamed like a mad dog, and gathered her to him with greedy jealousy. I did not feel as if I were in the company of a creature of my own species. . . . (ch. 15, p. 134)

Catherine is as necessary to the release of Heathcliff's feelings as he is to hers, and their mutual passion, with its intensity of a sexual climax, looks destructive to Nelly (Catherine seems dead), grotesque (Heathcliff foams like a mad dog), and unhuman. Nelly cannot understand it any more than she could Catherine's being Heathcliff. When Catherine says she is Heathcliff, she expresses a passion her society will not allow her to feel, and identifies the person her society will not allow her to be.

Modern readers tend to be more sympathetic to Catherine and Heathcliff than Nelly is, and we are more likely to put a positive value on their passion and energy, and to view negatively the restraints and limits of society. To most students and to many critics, Edgar Linton seems shadowy and pale next to Heathcliff, a milquetoast for whom Catherine deserts a Titan. But to disparage Edgar because he is not a Heathcliff, or the values of the Grange because they are not those of the Heights, is to commit the same error the characters make in the novel. Edgar, after all, loves Catherine and mourns her after her death, not as immoderately as Heathcliff does, but as sincerely. Catherine hopes to have half-a-dozen children by him (ch. 10, p. 93). Comparisons of the two men tend to reflect the reader's values and cultural training, rather than reveal Brontë's. Charlotte Brontë, in her preface to the 1850 edition of *Wuthering Heights,* approves highly of Edgar and wonders if it is advisable to create beings like Heathcliff. Charlotte's attitude is the modern error reversed. Emily makes no such judgment, but dramatizes a conflict which her heroine cannot solve because there is no basis on which a choice can be made—a fact that does not relieve Catherine from the necessity of choice. The men divide her being into what she is essentially, by nature, and what she becomes through the normal social growth of her personality. The novel's quest is to resolve this division into unity of being, a condition which Catherine yearns for in terms reminiscent of Brontë's best poetry: ". . . the thing that irks me most is this shattered prison, after all. I'm tired, tired of being enclosed here. I'm wearying to escape into that glorious world, and to be always there; not seeing it dimly through tears, and yearning for it through the walls of an aching heart; but really with it and in it" (ch. 15, p. 134). The wall of flesh which is her existence in this life bars her from that glorious existence without divisions in or limits to the self. Her grave will lie between Heathcliff's and Edgar's, and although, after all three are dead, villagers see her ghost only with Heathcliff's, she wears to the grave a locket into which Nelly has twisted together a dark strand of Heathcliff's hair and a light curl of Edgar's.

Nelly Dean: Point of View as One of the Divisions

Nelly is not often so even-handed in her treatment and descriptions of the characters. She identifies with the Lintons much more than with the Earnshaws, and prefers the moderate, civilized style of the Grange to the wild passion of the Heights. She admits that she does not like Catherine (ch. 8, p. 61); she does not want Edgar to yield to Catherine in their argument over Heathcliff (ch. 11, p. 102); she blames Catherine for bringing her illness "all on herself" (ch. 14, p. 124); and when Catherine faints, Nelly hopes that she is dead: "Far better that she should be dead, than lingering a burden and a misery-maker to all about her" (ch. 15, p. 136). Thus, while her narrative is entirely trustworthy as to its factual content, it is not an objective, disinterested account. Because Nelly's "heart invariably cleaved to the master's in preference to Catherine's side" (ch. 10, p. 93), her description of Catherine is sprinkled with negative epithets—words like "selfish," "haughty," "headstrong," "arrogant"—that have a cumulative, coercive effect on our view of Catherine. In telling the story to Lockwood, Nelly wants him to share her attitudes towards the characters; and though she is partial to young Cathy, she makes Lockwood reflect on the dangers of becoming involved with her, if the daughter should turn out "a second edition of the mother!" (ch. 14, p. 130).

There are a number of reasons why the reader must reject Nelly's interpretation of the story.[16] Her conventional, normal values and habits make her unfit to understand the violent extremes of Catherine and Heathcliff, and we have seen her pass judgment against Hindley because he does not conform to the values of Edgar. The divisions that make up the theme of the novel thus exist even between the tale and its teller. An emotional and conceptual gap separates Nelly sometimes from the most important events that she witnesses: Catherine's inner conflict, Heathcliff's psychic wounds. Nelly seldom questions her judgments, moreover, and she becomes in Brontë's hands a brilliant example of what we have come to call the unreliable narrator.

But Nelly, of course, does more than narrate the story from one side of it. She participates in events, and the action turns, at some critical moments, on what she does or fails to do. Nelly sees Heathcliff leave his place behind the settle when Catherine says it would degrade her to marry him, but she does not tell Catherine until it is too late to call Heathcliff back. The result is Catherine's serious illness. Later, at the Grange, she tells Edgar that Catherine and Heathcliff are arguing about the latter's behavior with Isabella, and she precipitates another crisis, after which Catherine becomes ill again. She agrees to function as Heathcliff's emissary to Catherine, delivers his letter to her, and helps to arrange their final meeting—which results in Catherine's death. Such a pattern, in which Nelly's actions have a consistently damaging effect on Catherine, coupled with Nelly's open dislike of her mistress, makes Nelly's motives a question of some importance. Nelly's word on the matter, the only explanation we are given, simply cannot be trusted, since Nelly tends to place herself in a favorable light, and does not examine her motives past the point which would be damaging to her. There is more behind her doings than what Nelly chooses or is able to tell.

A typical instance occurs when Edgar Linton comes to the Heights to court Catherine (ch. 8, pp. 64–66). The two expect to be left alone, but Nelly begins wiping the plate and cleaning drawers. She persistently ignores Catherine's commands to leave the room, and Catherine reacts violently, pinching Nelly on the arm. Nelly screams, Catherine denies having touched her, and Nelly exposes her lie by showing the bruise on her arm. All of this takes place in Edgar's presence, and when Edgar tries to calm Catherine, she slaps him. Nelly then says to herself, "Take warning and begone! It's a kindness to let you have a glimpse of her genuine disposition."

What is motivating Nelly in this scene? Why does she refuse to leave the room, and instead act in a way that she must know will light the short fuse of Catherine's temper? Nelly tells us only that Hindley had given her directions "to make a third party in any private visits Linton chose to pay"; but even if true—and this would be the only time either Hindley or Nelly show any interest in chaperoning Catherine—it tells nothing about Nelly's reasons, about her animosity towards Catherine and her sense of triumph at having made Catherine look bad. She obviously does not want the courtship to progress between Catherine and Edgar, and not because she wishes to do Edgar a kindness. She hardly knows him at this point. Nelly's actions are those of someone who is jealous or spiteful, who not only dislikes Catherine, but sees her as a rival. There is no suggestion of the two competing for the same lover—although it would not be unusual for a woman of twenty-two, with no man interested in her, to be jealous of Catherine's involvement with two men, at fifteen. But if their difference in rank rules out that rivalry, it raises the distinct possibility of another, one that goes far to explain Nelly's behavior. She wants to assert her equality to Catherine, even superiority over her, and is vying with Catherine for a place of power in the household.

Although Nelly is seven years older than Catherine and more sensible, Catherine is mistress and Nelly the servant. Nelly does not think of herself as a servant, however, and never acts, unless compelled to, in the role of an inferior. She tells Lockwood several times that she was Hindley's foster-sister, a relation that implies near or equal status to the Earnshaws, who for their part do not refer to Nelly as a foster-sister. One reason for her siding with the Lintons against the Earnshaws is that the Lintons' passiveness makes them more tractable to her: she can manage Edgar much more easily than she can Catherine or Heathcliff. When Catherine is in her last illness, Nelly almost has control over the Grange. Isabella remains, but again, whether they are calculated to do so or not, Nelly's actions result in the elimination of that possible rival. When Nelly discovers that Isabella has run off with Heathcliff, she decides not to tell Edgar. She gives as her reason the confusion already caused by Catherine's illness. She dare not rouse the family, and "still less unfold the business to my master, absorbed as he was in his present calamity, and having no heart to spare for a second grief!" (ch. 12, p. 112). Nelly is probably sincere, and she is not lying, but there is some question as to how deep the whole truth goes. She does not hesitate to initiate action at other times—as when she breaks off the correspondence between Linton Heathcliff and Cathy, without informing Edgar of their letters—and she could have directed some servants to pursue Isabella while there was still time to rescue her. Instead, by Nelly's keeping silent, Isabella marries Heathcliff and is banished from her home. After Catherine's death, Nelly becomes the virtual mistress of Thrushcross Grange.

James Hafley, who discusses these and other actions by Nelly, thinks the evidence is more than sufficient to pronounce Nelly the villain of the novel—a vicious, self-seeking woman who deceives Lockwood, and who has systematically destroyed or thwarted Catherine and Heathcliff.[17] His essay offers a challenging thesis, especially to those who take Nelly's judgments to have the authority of reason and common sense. But to make Nelly—or Heathcliff or Hindley—the villain of *Wuthering Heights* reduces its moral vision to a single system of good and evil, whereas what we find are different, opposing systems. Nelly emerges as the chief proponent of the system that belongs to the Grange; Heathcliff, the only other major character besides Nelly to play an active role in both generations, embodies the value system of the Heights. Their careers, in fact, are parallel. Both begin as servants and rise to become master and mistress of their respective homes, in fact if not in law. Both are strong-willed and resourceful; both acquire manners and learning unusual for their class and origin. Each can be ruthless. Heathcliff lets his son die for want of medical attention. Nelly simply omits telling Edgar that his wife has been starving herself for three days. A power struggle between them underlies the second half of the novel, and emerges as a clash of wills when Heathcliff imprisons Nelly and Cathy at the Heights. Cathy is desperate to return to the dying Edgar, and Nelly vows, "Her father *shall* see her . . . if that devil be killed on his own doorstones in trying to prevent it!" (ch. 28, p. 225). Nelly is the only one of the Linton faction who has the strength to stand up to the Earnshaws, who is undaunted by them; and without her to even the balance, the conflict between the two houses would probably be one-sided. With her it is a seesaw. After Edgar's death, Heathcliff deposes her from her position at the Grange; after Heathcliff's death, Nelly will reinstate herself there with Cathy and Hareton.

The parallels between them suggest that there is a common point of identity between Heathcliff and Nelly—as there is between Heathcliff and Edgar, when he strikes Heathcliff in the throat; Isabella, when she covets Hindley's gun; and Lockwood when he dreams. The Grange people tend to suppress and be unconscious of their mutual identity with one who seems to them a principle of evil—Nelly's "devil." Heathcliff, for his part, rejects even his son because he has the Linton name and features. Seeing each other only as opposites, and failing to recognize the existence they have in common, the two houses join only in a destructive state of violence.

But the primal condition of life for Brontë is a unity that overcomes or dissolves conflict and division.[18] Both houses, not one or the other, comprise the microcosm of existence, and each house supplies for the other a fullness of life which alone it cannot have—completes its circumference of being to make one circle of life. Brontë's vision of this, of the relation of the two houses to each other, is best represented, I think, by the Taoist symbol of Yang and Yin, the two principles which comprise the whole of existence.

One is light, active, masculine; the other is dark, passive, feminine.[19] Yet the light is not all light, but contains darkness; and the darkness is not all dark, but contains light. The same can be said of Earnshaw and Linton, the Heights and the Grange. Members of the second generation, after the violence and polarization of the first, find their way to that truth.

Towards Unity of Being

As we know, Catherine dies halfway through the novel, and Brontë virtually begins the story again, using a second group of characters to reconstruct a triangle like that of the first generation, their parents. Cathy Linton takes the place of her mother. She is attracted to the fair appearance and cultivated manners of Linton Heathcliff, who, though he is the son of Heathcliff, resembles Edgar, from whom he will inherit the Grange. Linton Heathcliff is a skillfully drawn, grotesque figure in whom weakness produces ruthlessness. It is through his presence and death that the destructive elements of the first generation are purged, for he combines, as David Cecil points out, all the negative traits of the first generation—Heathcliff's cruelty, the Lintons' cowardice—and thus the stronger, positive traits can descend to Hareton and Cathy.[20] Hareton Earnshaw, the son of Heathcliff's oppressor, Hindley, takes on the role of Heathcliff, and is heir to the Heights. Cathy's progress from one to the other reverses the pattern set by her mother. Catherine went from the Heights and identification with Heathcliff to the Grange and marriage to Edgar. Cathy goes from the Grange to the Heights, from marriage to Linton to identification with Hareton. Also, as Catherine learns social manners at the Grange, Cathy becomes fierce and unrelenting at the Heights. Together, the two women encompass a cycle of identity, a full circle in which the three names Catherine carved on her window ledge come into being: Catherine Earnshaw, Catherine Linton, Catherine Heathcliff.

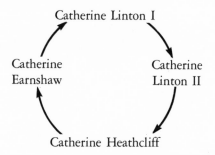

Catherine Linton I

Catherine Earnshaw

Catherine Linton II

Catherine Heathcliff

Moreover, the underlying unity of being that eludes the first generation appears more directly in the second, for these are crossbreeds, the joining of a Linton or an Earnshaw (Heathcliff) with its opposite. They are the combination, that is, of the forces that threw the first generation into conflict—the forces tending toward socialization and the law, the forces tending toward individuality and freedom. For life, as *Wuthering Heights* conceives it, to continue, the two forces must be brought from opposition to harmony, and the cycle begun by the division of the first Catherine complete itself in the wholeness of the second.

Catherine's division was between two centers of existence, one vital, one valuable; she could not choose to stay with Heathcliff or marry Edgar without forfeiting a part of her self. Both of them love her. Cathy's choices, on the other hand, are between a clearly unfit and a fit partner: the selfish Linton, who lives an unvital, contracted life, and the loving Hareton, with whom she can share a vital, expansive life. But whereas her mother clearly saw the nature of her dilemma though she could not solve it, Cathy is deceived, and she mistakes appearances for reality. She admires Linton at first, and only gradually learns to see his cruel, almost repulsive nature, and the enormity of his fear. His frailty and dependence on her had made her protective of him, but when he falls to her feet in utter terror of his father, Cathy is awakened to his true nature and is repulsed by it. "Rise, and don't degrade yourself into an abject reptile," she pleads (ch. 27, p. 212). Forced on her by Heathcliff, her marriage to Linton is a marriage with death: Linton is impotent in every sense of the term, there is no love between them now, and Cathy's world is falling to pieces. After the long hours of caring for him, when Linton dies, Cathy says with a bitterness she couldn't conceal, "you have left me so long to struggle against death, alone, that I feel and see only death! I feel like death!" (ch. 30, p. 233). She is at her nadir, the point from which she rises to gain a true perception of Hareton, whom she had at first thought repulsive and learns to admire.

This is also the point in the story at which the novel begins. When Lockwood visits the Heights in chapter 2, Cathy and Hareton are carrying on the opposition and polarity that divided the first generation. When Lockwood leaves the area for London, the two remaining cousins seem enmeshed and separated by the web of their parents' lives. By the time of Lockwood's final visit, the two have ended their war and found peace.

In this final movement of the novel, Hareton begins as the Earnshaw principle reduced to its most uncivilized and ignorant state. At five years old, he strikes Nelly with a stone, accompanied by "a string of curses, which, whether he comprehended them or not, were delivered with practised emphasis, and distorted his baby features into a shocking expression of malignity" (ch. 11, p. 95). Later, talking to him as she would to one of the stable boys at the Grange, Cathy cannot accept the fact that he is her cousin (ch. 18, p. 160). Hareton cannot read, and as he, Cathy, and Linton stand outside the door of Wuthering Heights, Cathy asks him the meaning of the inscription over the door. Lockwood had read it in chapter 1, and it is Hareton's name, with the date 1500:

> Hareton stared up, and scratched his head like a true clown.
>
> "It's some damnable writing," he answered. "I cannot read it."
>
> "Can't read it?" cried Catherine; "I can read it: it's English. But I want to know why it is there."
>
> Linton giggled—the first appearance of mirth he had exhibited.
>
> "He does not know his letters," he said to his cousin. "Could you believe in the existence of such a colossal dunce?"
>
> "Is he all as he should be?" asked Miss Cathy seriously, "or is he simple—not right? I've questioned him twice now, and each time he looked so stupid I think he does not understand me; I can hardly understand *him,* I'm sure!" (ch. 21, pp. 178–79)

Brontë wants us to notice the cruelty of their class snobbery, but Hareton's ignorance and limitations are real—he is tongue-tied, dumb. Cathy's hostility towards him makes her unjust to his essentially good nature and feelings, but she is not wrong about the state of his mind. After her feelings begin to change, and she wants his companionship, she describes him to Nelly: "He's just like a dog, is he not . . . or a cart-horse? He does his work, eats his food, and sleeps, eternally! What a blank, dreary mind he must have! Do you ever dream, Hareton? And if you do, what is it about? But you can't speak to me!" (ch. 32, p. 245).

Hareton's development is from this brutish, blank state of mind—Heathcliff's state when Catherine asks him, "What do you talk about?"—toward the civilization and refinement he associates with Cathy. Attracted to her, he wants to emulate her, bring his self closer to hers. He begins teaching himself to read, and discovers the meaning of the letters over the door—his name and the mark of his identity, which he now comes into a more complete possession of. His development is slow—as Nelly says, Hareton was not to be civilized with a wish—and involves clashes with the hostile Cathy, but in the last third of the novel, as Hareton moves toward the civilized life symbolized by the ability to read, his life becomes more expansive and free. He has a mental awakening to himself, to his, the Earnshaw, past, and to the past embodied in literature. He gains a greater physical freedom, and digs up Joseph's old trees to plant flowers imported from the Grange in their place. He learns to laugh. As the Linton principle—the values of the Grange—becomes manifest in Hareton, the effect is the reverse of what it was felt to be in the first generation: a widening rather than a restriction of his being. For Hareton, the socializing process has become a liberating process, not its opposite.

If it takes time for Hareton to acquire the values of the Grange, Cathy is just as slow to allow them to one from the Heights. Although as a girl, she refused to be bound within the walls of the Grange—"The Grange is not a prison," she tells Nelly, "and you are not my jailer" (ch. 23, p. 195)—her removal to the Heights deprives her of the only form of society she has known, and makes her bitter. She is sullen and rude even to Lockwood. In her infatuation with Linton Heathcliff, she considers Hareton contemptible, beneath her notice: he is a "brute." His learning to read his name draws only mockery from her (ch. 24, p. 200). After a quarrel, when Hareton stops her horse on the way out of the Heights, to apologize and explain, Cathy cuts him off by striking him with her whip. When she is settled at the Heights, after Linton has died, she discovers a stock of books in Hareton's room, some of them her own and brought from the Grange. She accuses Hareton of having gathered them "as a magpie gathers silver spoons, for the mere love of stealing! They are of no use to you; or else you concealed them in the bad spirit, that as you cannot enjoy them, nobody else shall" (ch. 31, p. 238). She mimics his blundering attempts to read poetry, and finally

makes Hareton so angry he throws the books into the fire. "That's all
the good that such a brute as you can get from them," Cathy cries (ch.
31, p. 239). As Lockwood accurately perceives, Hareton had learned to
read to please Cathy and bridge the division between them. She sees it
only as an affront to herself and her class privilege.

Cathy's society has shrunk to herself, and its values have become
mental walls that keep Hareton out, as the walls of the Grange had kept
her in. Her development is to remove the barrier of her attitudes and
create a new society by accepting Hareton as himself and her cousin. She
wants to converse with him, and realizes that he won't answer her
because she has laughed at him before. She persists in seeking his
company, because there is no one else for her to share life with, and
because, as she says, "I've found out, Hareton, that I want—that I'm
glad—that I should like you to be my cousin, now . . ." (ch. 32, p.
247). To heal the wounds she inflicted, she wraps a handsome book in
white paper, ties it with a ribbon, and addresses it to "Mr. Hareton
Earnshaw" (ch. 32, p. 248)—thus acknowledging his identity and
atoning for the mockery with which she met his first reading of his
name. The "Mr." is her formal acceptance of Hareton into her world as
her equal. Thus, as the civilization of Hareton frees him from a prison of
mental darkness, Cathy escapes the prison of her class prejudices by
accepting Hareton's individuality. The society on which the Linton
principle rests is made possible by the inclusion of an Earnshaw.[21]

The two enemies can become one family, however, because Heathcliff does not oppose them, and because as they are finding one solution
to the novel's conflict, he reaches another. A "strange change," as
Heathcliff calls it, is coming over him (ch. 33, p. 255). Having
obtained power over both houses, so that by a single effort he could
destroy them, he has become indifferent to their destruction, has "lost
the faculty of enjoying their destruction." Always enigmatic to others,
in his prolonged rage as in this change, Heathcliff is made more
complex by what happens to Hareton. Brontë does not allow us, that is,
to make heredity or environment the determining influence on Heathcliff's character, because they do not account for Hareton's. Heathcliff's
parentage is unknown and probably unimportant, since Hareton has
none of the brutal traits of his father, Hindley. Environment is a more
visible factor. We see Hindley abusing Heathcliff, who vows and gets
revenge. But even before Hindley becomes master of the Heights, and
when Heathcliff is old Mr. Earnshaw's favorite, he is a sullen, unrespon-

sive child. More importantly, Hareton suffers the same treatment as Heathcliff, without its having a lasting effect on his nature. A hateful environment cannot be primarily responsible for the hatred in Heathcliff, since the same conditions result in Hareton's love—not only for Cathy, but for Heathcliff as well.

Brontë may well have begun with one conception of Heathcliff and then shifted to others, as Q. D. Leavis suggests.[22] But the intervening points of view which Brontë puts between the reader and Heathcliff suggest that she was in control of her art and used the device to make her readers aware of the necessity and difficulty of seeing Heathcliff himself, apart from his image in the minds of others, and to challenge us to partake in his perception, although we can only approach it from theirs. To others, the Lintons and Nelly especially, Heathcliff seems a fiercely physical man, or spawn of the devil, whereas his own attention is directed toward some undefinable spiritual realm, where he can sense the presence of Catherine's ghost. Besides Catherine, other people scarcely exist for Heathcliff, or they come into his notice only as obstacles to her or as reminders of his loss. The torment of not being able to see or touch the one thing that matters to his feelings makes him violent to others, but almost oblivious of them as well. The center of their existence—the focus of ordinary life—is on the periphery of his, just as the center of his life, his perceptions, differs greatly from theirs. The difference, another of the divisions of the novel, is nowhere more apparent than in two accounts of the same event as experienced by Isabella and Heathcliff.

Isabella's version comes first (ch. 17, pp. 144–48), and is graphic in its description of violence. It is the evening of Catherine's funeral, and Hindley, resolved to kill Heathcliff if he reenters the Heights, has locked the doors and windows, and waits with the pistol that has a knife attached to its barrel. The atmosphere is tense and climactic. Isabella warns Heathcliff and taunts him; Hindley swears passionately at both; Heathcliff bursts open a window casement, but cannot get through the narrow frame. "His hair and clothes were whitened with snow, and his sharp cannibal teeth, revealed by cold and wrath, gleamed through the dark." Hindley rushes to the window, but before he can use his weapon, Heathcliff wrenches it from his hand:

The charge exploded, and the knife, in springing back, closed into its owner's wrist. Heathcliff pulled it away by main force, slitting up the flesh as it passed on, and thrust it dripping into his pocket. He then took a stone, struck down the division between two windows, and sprung in. His adversary had fallen senseless with excessive pain and the flow of blood that gushed from an artery, or a large vein.

The ruffian kicked and trampled on him, and dashed his head repeatedly against the flags, holding me with one hand, meantime, to prevent me summoning Joseph. (ch. 17, p. 147)

When Joseph arrives, Heathcliff shakes Isabella until her teeth rattle, and throws her beside Joseph, who is praying on the floor.

Isabella's account comprises an entire episode, almost four pages long in the Norton Critical Edition. She perceives Heathcliff acting maliciously and deliberately to inflict the greatest possible hurt to Hindley, without killing him. There is no reason to doubt what she sees, but for Heathcliff the evening is memorable for entirely different reasons and for its associations with a different scene. It was that night, after he had dug to Catherine's coffin, that he felt her presence by her grave. The fight with Hindley is only a minor interruption in his search to find Catherine, and he describes it in three sentences. "Having reached the Heights, I rushed eagerly to the door. It was fastened; and, I remember, that accursed Earnshaw and my wife opposed my entrance. I remember stopping to kick the breath out of him, and then hurrying upstairs, to my room, and hers" (ch. 29, p. 230). In Isabella's account everything is made vivid and visible; for Heathcliff, the episode marks the beginning of his quest for the invisible. His real struggle is with Catherine's ghost.

Dead, Catherine is no less real to Heathcliff than she was alive. But she exists for him now as an image of perfection, as his soul, which he can imagine but no longer see and must relentlessly pursue. Brontë's conception of his quest—his inability to value the world Catherine has left, his goal of seeing her again—connects *Wuthering Heights* to such Romantic poems as Byron's "Manfred," Shelley's "Alastor," and Keats's "Endymion." Brontë's Romanticism is well known, and her poems are frequently discussed in conjunction with Blake's. She was a visionary. Heathcliff, in effect, becomes one; and at the end, when he seems weirdest of all to Nelly, he is living in an imaginative world, mostly, and only incidentally in the world of the senses. The strange change coming over him is a spiritualization of his being, the dissolution of his tie to his physical self. Still strong and in his thirties, he does not anticipate dying, yet his own body seems more foreign to him than death. "I cannot continue in this condition," he says. "I have to remind myself to breathe—almost to remind my heart to beat! And it is like bending back a stiff spring; it is by compulsion that I do the slightest act not prompted by one thought, and by compulsion, that I notice anything alive, or dead, which is not associated with one universal idea. I have a single wish, and my whole being and faculties are yearning to attain it" (ch. 33, p. 256). The "thought," the "universal idea" contained in Catherine "has devoured [his] existence." Like the visionary A. G. Rochelle, Heathcliff's "outward sense is gone, [his] inward essence feels";[23] and the invisible becomes visible to him as it did to Rochelle: he can see Catherine three feet away from him. But whereas Rochelle suffers the loss of her vision when her eye begins to see again and the physical world asserts its claim on her, Heathcliff's soul is almost free. It is only with difficulty that he can direct his attention to physical things. He has gained a peace that is very similar to Brontë's in her last mystical poems: without leaving the earth, he is "nearly" in "heaven" (ch. 34, p. 263).

Wuthering Heights ends with its divisions healed and its conflicts over. Yet it ends ambiguously, without putting a final limit to the meaning of what it has told, or to life's possibilities. We last "see" Heathcliff and Catherine through the eyes of a shepherd boy, who is frightened by their ghosts on the moors. The union of Heathcliff and Catherine takes place at the same time, or very nearly the same, as the union of Hareton and Cathy. On his last visit to the Heights, Lockwood sees them by one of the windows, where Cathy is teaching Hareton to read. Earnshaw restlessness in the ghosts and Linton domesticity persist, and these last scenes are a throwback to that early scene when Heathcliff and Catherine first wander across the moors to the Grange, where they see two children in the window. But then Edgar and Isabella were fighting, and Catherine and Heathcliff were attacked by the dog. In the peace that reigns now, the two pairs can follow their separate ways without interference or danger from each other—although Heathcliff and Catherine will become a part of their area's myth to haunt someone like Joseph.

Although their mystical marriage is their private heaven—or perhaps because it is—Brontë accomplishes more through the domestic marriage of Cathy and Hareton. They solve the triangular conflict of Edgar, Catherine, and Heathcliff. Cathy, as we saw, takes on the role of her mother. She bears her mother's name, has her mother's eyes and spirit, and completes the cycle begun by her mother. We can say, then, that she is the symbol of Catherine's presence. Hareton is the second Heathcliff; his upbringing has been a deliberate repetition of Heathcliff's. "Five minutes ago, Hareton seemed a personification of my youth," Heathcliff says (ch. 33, p. 255). Hareton thinks of Heathcliff as his father and loves him as such. Thus, in the persons of Cathy and Hareton, we have the marriage of a second Catherine and a second Heathcliff. But Cathy is a Linton, and says herself that she is closest to her father. Except for her eyes, she resembles Edgar, and she has inherited his values, so that she is the symbol of his presence, too. Hareton is an Earnshaw and resembles, not his father, but Catherine, his aunt. Both Nelly and Heathcliff remark on Hareton's "startling likeness to Catherine" (ch. 33, p. 255). He is the symbol of her presence. In the persons of Hareton and Cathy, then, we have the marriage of a second Catherine and a second Edgar. Hareton = Catherine, and Hareton = Heathcliff; Cathy = Edgar, and Cathy = Catherine. This set of equations, admittedly tentative, would mean that the one marriage between Hareton and Cathy contains the two marriages that were not both possible in the first generation:

(Catherine)	x	(Edgar)
Hareton	x	Cathy
(Heathcliff)	x	(Catherine)

And even if Brontë did not intend that tight a unity, it is the impression of the living couple on Lockwood's mind that makes him wonder, when he is standing at the graves of the other three, "how any one could ever imagine unquiet slumbers for the sleepers in that quiet earth."

Chapter Six

Conclusion

Because it seems to epitomize Emily Brontë's vision, I have reserved one of her poems for discussion in this conclusion. *Wuthering Heights,* of course, is her masterpiece; the following lines give a condensed image of the mind that produced it. They show us the training of an artist, as Brontë learns the compassionate honesty that characterizes her best work.

> "Well, some may hate, and some may scorn,
> And some may quite forget thy name,
> But my sad heart must ever mourn
> Thy ruined hopes, thy blighted fame."
>
> 'Twas thus I thought, an hour ago,
> Even weeping o'er that wretch's woe.
> One word turned back my gushing tears,
> And lit my altered eye with sneers.
>
> "Then bless the friendly dust," I said,
> "That hides thy unlamented head.
> Vain as thou wert, and weak as vain,
> The slave of falsehood, pride and pain,
> My heart has nought akin to thine—
> Thy soul is powerless over mine."
>
> But these were thoughts that vanished too—
> Unwise, unholy, and untrue—
> Do I despise the timid deer
> Because his limbs are fleet with fear?
> Or would I mock the wolf's death-howl
> Because his form is gaunt and foul?
> Or hear with joy the leveret's cry
> Because it cannot bravely die?

No! Then above his memory
Let pity's heart as tender be:
Say, "Earth lie lightly on that breast,
And, kind Heaven, grant that spirit rest!"
                    (*Complete Poems*, #123, pp. 132–33)

Dated November 14, 1839, the poem was included with her personal writings, when Brontë copied her poems into the two notebooks of 1844. We can, even knowing Brontë's penchant for masks, assume the voice to be hers. It tells us that she both refused to falsify reality and did not refuse her sympathy to whatever forms reality took. The first of these requires an unflinching honesty; the second, compassion. In "Well, some may hate," Brontë learns to join compassion and honesty, after proving the inadequacy of each without the other.

The poem has a dialectical pattern in which Brontë develops from a shallow compassion for someone, to a disillusioned rejection of him, to a full understanding. In the first two stanzas, Brontë expresses grief, but in conventional and borrowed terms, clichés, such as "sad heart" and "gushing tears." This is not the honest language of her feelings, for she is resentful of and angry at this "wretch" who, in his apparently dissolute life, has wounded her. Thus, while her grief seems to set her apart from those who hate and scorn the other, it only conceals feelings in her that are similar to theirs. This fact becomes apparent in the third stanza, where Brontë's indignation erupts to reject the other in harsh moral terms: "Vain as thou wert, and weak as vain, / The slave of falsehood, pride and pain." As she admits the truth about the other's character, the feelings about him she can no longer deny displace the shallower sentiments of the opening. Her heart has severed from his. Yet it is now, when she has faced the truth, that the third movement begins toward a new and more honest sympathy. The accusatory mind fades, as "Unwise, unholy, and untrue"; Brontë had been judging the other by the pain he caused her, rather than by the suffering he brought on himself. She had been misled by her attitude of moral superiority to the other, whom she saw, first, as someone needing her forgiveness, and second, as someone deserving her condemnation. Now she understands him as he exists independently of her forgiveness and censure, like the deer and the wolf. Brontë's acquired vision is a form of detachment, not from the other, but from her self, for it brings her closer to the other. She is aware that one can create his own hell, but she condemns no one to hell.

We do not know who it was—whether a real or an imaginary person—Brontë addressed in "Well, some may hate." But the poem can guide us to what she probably thought about Branwell in his last years, and more importantly, it can suggest how she saw the violent, lawless people of Gondal and *Wuthering Heights*. Heathcliff especially challenges our moral sensibilities because we cannot overlook the fact that, although he is a symbolic figure who attains his own version of salvation or heaven, for most of his life he acts savagely and even sadistically against others. He hurts his enemies and enjoys their suffering, deciding himself that they deserve to suffer. Even Catherine Earnshaw, who is partial *to* Heathcliff, calls him a "fierce, pitiless, wolfish man" (ch. 10, p. 90). Brontë is not indifferent to the moral questions Heathcliff raises. She is aware of the evil of his actions and knows Heathcliff is wrong to let his son die when Heathcliff no longer needs him—the daughter of an Anglican minister would know what sin is. Yet, in her eyes, the acts and the sins do not condemn the man, nor do they move her to forgive him. They make her aware of the man's necessities, the irreducible nature or self-ness of a Heathcliff, or a Catherine, or an Augusta Almeda. Brontë's characters act as their natures compel them to act, and while Christian or Western codes apply to a judgment of the actions, the irreducible self is unique to itself, like the deer or the wolf: another's forgiveness or censure can neither redeem nor condemn it. The best, the most moral response under such conditions would be to perceive and respect each other's necessities, so that there will be harmony and not conflict between the selves we cannot help but be. Brontë did not say that directly, of course, but I think it is an inescapable implication of her work—it is what her work shows. The moral strength of her imagination was its ability to understand, without having to rank or judge the different necessities in the irreducible selves it created or found.

Unknown at her death, when her poetry was ignored and her novel misunderstood, Emily Brontë now ranks with the foremost writers of her time; and though she published very little, by Victorian standards especially, no one can ignore her who is interested in the creative imagination, the history of the novel, or the possibilities of lyric poetry. Her popular appeal, of course, cannot be separated from that of the whole Brontë family. Their Haworth home, officially a museum, has become a shrine which Brontë enthusiasts now visit in numbers of well over 100,000 a year.

The Brontë cult was already strong in the nineteenth century, but it was centered mostly on Charlotte, and for seventy years after the Brontë's brief public career, Emily was regarded and written about more as Charlotte's sister than as an author in her own right. Serious criticism of *Wuthering Heights* did not begin until the 1920s. Earlier, readers of *Wuthering Heights* were generally either uncritically rhapsodic in their praise of its power, or disgusted at its violence, or apologetic for what was thought to be its technical defects and bad writing.[1] A shift in attitude is apparent by 1924, when literary values and critical expectations had been changed by the innovations and technical experiments of the modernists—Conrad, Joyce, Woolf—and by the violence of a world war. In that year, Lascelles Abercrombie could assert confidently that Emily was the greatest of the Brontës. The "unquestionable supremacy of Emily" is "obvious" to him in the way the Brontës "appear to us today."[2] Sanger's close study of the structure of *Wuthering Heights*, in 1926, revealed the painstaking care with which Brontë planned and constructed her novel; and what had seemed a powerful but crude tale to the Victorians and their immediate successors became a rich source for the study of symbolism, irony, and myth by the 1950s. Surely, few Victorian novels have attracted more attention among all levels of readers for the past fifty years than has *Wuthering Heights*. If F. B. Pinion is correct, by the mid-1970s *Wuthering Heights* had "elicited more critical essays than all the other Brontë novels."[3]

Yet, of the three fated and tragic Brontë sisters, Emily is still the least known and the most mysterious. The story of her life, like the history of the Gondalans, can only be inferred from scattered fragments and glimpses. For a brief moment, on a November afternoon, a sixteen-year-old girl appears in the Haworth kitchen, watching with her eyes Sally Mosley doing the laundry, while her mind sees the Gondals discovering Gaaldine. Later she appears in other brief scenes—as The Major chaperoning Ellen Nussey and Patrick Brontë's new curate; or as an actress playing Juliet Augusteena and Henry Angora on a trip to York; or as a poet angry because her secret manuscripts have been read;

or as Ellis Bell pacing the parlor floor with Currer and Acton. And we know little more, except that for all this time she was a storyteller whose private, secret myths prepared her to write one of the most passionate novels in the language, and that she became an artist who learned to master the dispassionate discipline of her craft. Her poetry, which is only now receiving the attention it deserves, was read and appreciated by Emily Dickinson. In his elegy to the Brontës, "Haworth Churchyard," Matthew Arnold recalls the emotions "No Coward Soul" awoke in him. And in a prophetic moment, Swinburne said of *Wuthering Heights* that those who do like it "will like nothing very much better in the whole world of poetry and prose."[4] Emily Brontë now belongs to the world, but it is fitting that poets should have been among the very first to recognize her power. The poetic or creative imagination, as Brontë knew, is the most demanding and active; she lived, as fully and as purely as she could, the life it made necessary for her.

Notes and References

Chapter One

1. Elizabeth Gaskell, *The Life of Charlotte Brontë,* Everyman's Library Edition (London, n.d.), p. 36.
2. Ellen Nussey, "Reminiscences of Charlotte Brontë," *Scribner's Monthly* 2 (May 1871):26–27.
3. Ibid., p. 27.
4. Annette B. Hopkins, *The Father of the Brontës* (Baltimore: The Johns Hopkins Press, 1958), pp. 28, 32.
5. Gaskell, p. 31.
6. Charlotte Brontë, "The History of the Year," in *The Miscellaneous and Unpublished Writings of Charlotte and Patrick Branwell Brontë in Two Volumes,* ed. T. J. Wise and J. A. Symington (Oxford, 1936), I:2.
7. Francis A. Leyland, *The Brontë Family, With Special Reference to Patrick Branwell Brontë* (London: Hurst and Blackett, 1886), 1:63–64.
8. Fannie Elizabeth Ratchford, *The Brontës' Web of Childhood* (New York, 1941), p. 7.
9. Charlotte Brontë, "The History of the Year," p. 1.
10. Ratchford, pp. 18–19.
11. This is the text of the diary note as it appears in Winifred Gérin, *Emily Brontë, A Biography* (Oxford, 1971), p. 39.
12. *The Complete Poems of Emily Jane Brontë,* ed. C. W. Hatfield (New York, 1941), p. 29.
13. Clement Shorter, *The Brontës: Life and Letters* (London, 1908), 1:94; hereafter cited as *Life and Letters.*
14. Mrs. Ellis H. Chadwick, *In the Footsteps of the Brontës* (London, 1914), p. 124.
15. Charlotte Brontë's preface first appears in the 1850 edition of *Wuthering Heights,* and the portion quoted is reprinted by Hilda Marsden and Ian Jack, eds., in The Clarendon Edition of *Wuthering Heights* (Oxford, 1976), p. 446.
16. *The Complete Poems of Emily Jane Brontë,* pp. 93–95.
17. Gérin, p. 62.
18. Ibid., p. 65.
19. *Life and Letters,* 1:138. I have accepted Winifred Gérin's date for this letter (*Emily Brontë, A Biography,* p. 70), but a number of sources, including

Gaskell and Chadwick, date it a year earlier. The date given in *Life and Letters*—April 2, 1837—is clearly erroneous.

20. Gérin, p. 84.

21. Leyland, 1:153–54.

22. Chadwick, p. 126.

23. The orphan was named Jack Sharp. Gérin gives his history in full in *Emily Brontë, A Biography,* pp. 76–80.

24. *The Complete Poems of Emily Jane Brontë,* p. 63.

25. A. Mary F. Robinson (afterwards Madame Duclaux), *Emily Brontë,* 2nd ed., Eminent Women Series (London, 1889), p. 51.

26. Ibid., pp. 53–54.

27. Gaskell, pp. 184–85.

28. *Life and Letters,* 1:216.

29. Ibid., p. 224.

30. Gérin, pp. 119, 121.

31. *Life and Letters,* 1:237.

32. Gaskell, p. 147.

33. Ibid., p. 152.

34. Ibid., p. 151.

35. Gérin, pp. 137–38.

36. Ibid., p. 142.

37. Ibid., pp. 147–48.

38. *Life and Letters,* 1:304–305.

39. Ibid., p. 307.

40. Ibid., p. 306.

41. Charlotte Brontë's 1850 "Biographical Notice of Ellis and Acton Bell" is frequently reprinted. I have used the Norton Critical Edition of *Wuthering Heights,* ed. William M. Sale, Jr. (New York, 1963), p. 4.

42. Gérin, p. 184.

43. *Life and Letters,* 1:325.

44. Gaskell, p. 215.

45. Gérin, p. 209.

46. Muriel Spark and Derek Stanford, *Emily Brontë, Her Life and Work* (New York, 1966), p. 87.

47. *Life and Letters,* 1:442.

48. Ibid., p. 336.

49. Robinson, p. 125.

50. Gérin, pp. 242–45.

51. See Laura Hinkley, *The Brontës: Charlotte and Emily* (London, 1947), p. 119; and *Life and Letters,* 1:321.

52. Robinson, pp. 126–27.

53. Gaskell, p. 198.

Chapter Two

1. C. W. Hatfield lists six manuscript and three printed sources for Emily Brontë's poems in *The Complete Poems of Emily Jane Brontë,* ed. C. W. Hatfield (New York, 1941), pp. 24–26.

2. Clement Shorter, *The Brontës: Life and Letters* (London, 1908), 1:304–307.

3. Muriel Spark and Derek Stanford, *Emily Brontë: Her Life and Work* (New York, 1966), p. 121.

4. Laura Hinkley, *The Brontës: Charlotte and Emily* (London, 1947), p. 274. For Hinkley's reconstruction of the Gondal story, see Appendix A, pp. 273–82.

5. Fannie E. Ratchford, *Gondal's Queen: A Novel in Verse by Emily Jane Brontë* (Austin, 1955), pp. 26–27.

6. W. D. Paden, *An Investigation of Gondal* (New York, 1958), passim.

7. Fannie E. Ratchford, *The Brontë's Web of Childhood* (New York, 1941), p. 103. Ratchford's source is a list of Gondalan place names made by Anne.

8. Ibid., p. 257.

9. Ratchford gives a somewhat different version of the dramatis personae in *Gondal's Queen,* pp. 43–44. Paden, in *An Investigation of Gondal,* constructs a genealogical diagram of the relationships between the various characters and families. See p. 51.

10. This information is contained in a poem entitled "From a Dungeon Wall in the Southern College," to which is added: "E. J. B., Nov. 11, 1844/ J. B., Sept., 1825." *The Complete Poems of Emily Jane Brontë,* #178, pp. 212–14. Not all of Brontë's poems have titles, and all further references to her poetry will be given in the text by both the entry number and the page number in Hatfield's edition.

11. Ratchford, *Gondal's Queen,* pp. 105–106.

12. See the genealogical chart in Paden, *An Investigation of Gondal,* p. 51. In a poem entitled "A. S. to G. S.," the speaker (unnamed, though almost certainly Alfred) consoles one he names Gerald for the death of their mother. *The Complete Poems,* #152, pp. 172–73.

13. Brontë's arrangement of the poems in this notebook does not follow the order of their composition, but rather suggests the chronological order of the events in Gondal.

14. I accept Paden's argument for the identity of Alexandria. See *An Investigation of Gondal,* pp. 45–50.

15. The poem in which Blanche describes her journey to Gaaldine with her young nursling exists in two versions, both written May 1838. In one, the child is described as "dark haired," and in the other as "bright haired." *The Complete Poems,* #62, pp. 71–72.

16. Ratchford, *Gondal's Queen,* p. 32.

17. See the Appendix in Mary Visick, *The Genesis of Wuthering Heights* (Hong Kong, 1958), pp. 83–86.

18. Spark and Stanford, pp. 120–35.

19. Paden, p. 39; Ratchford, *Gondal's Queen,* p. 128.

Chapter Three

1. Charlotte Brontë, "Biographical Notice of Ellis and Acton Bell," in *Wuthering Heights,* ed. William M. Sale, Jr. (New York, 1963), p. 4. Because of the many different editions of *Wuthering Heights,* references to the novel will include chapter number as well as the page number in this, the Norton Critical Edition.

2. Some excellent, thorough criticism of Brontë's poems can be found in Inga-Stina Ewbank, *Their Proper Sphere: A Study of the Brontë Sisters as Early-Victorian Female Novelists* (London, 1966), pp. 86–155; and in Muriel Spark and Derek Stanford, pp. 136–221. Stanford is generally more il-luminating about Brontë's flawed poems than he is about what he considers to be her six completely successful poems. Three of the essays in *The Art of Emily Brontë,* ed. Anne Smith (New York: Barnes and Noble Books, 1976), concern themselves with Brontë's poetry: Robin Grove, " 'It Would Not Do': Emily Brontë as Poet," pp. 33–67; Rosalind Miles, "A Baby God: The Creative Dynamism of Emily Brontë's Poetry," pp. 68–93; and Barbara Hardy, "The Lyricism of Emily Brontë," pp. 94–118. Each offers insightful readings of individual poems.

3. See Richard B. Sewall, *The Life of Emily Dickinson* (New York: Farrar, Straus and Giroux, 1974), 2:621. "No coward soul is mine" was one of Dickinson's favorite poems.

4. *The Complete Poems of Emily Jane Brontë,* ed. C. W. Hatfield (New York, 1941). All further references to Brontë's poems will be given in the text by both the entry number and the page number in Hatfield's edition.

5. Charles Morgan, *Reflections in a Mirror* (London, 1944), p. 136. C. Day Lewis, "Emily Brontë and Freedom," *Notable Images of Virtue* (Toronto, 1954), p. 6, assumes that "I am the only being whose doom" is spoken in Brontë's own voice; and Rosalind Miles claims that this is true of Brontë's poetry as a whole: "Hers is a ventriloquial gift, not a dramatic one" ("A Baby God: The Creative Dynamism of Emily Brontë's Poetry," p. 76). Denis Donoghue, who also hears "a kind of ventriloquism" in Brontë's poetry,

states the problem of identifying Brontë's speakers most succinctly when he says that her poetry falls somewhere between dramatic monologue and soliloquy, and that we do not have a precise term for it. See his "Emily Brontë: On the Latitude of Interpretation," *The Interpretation of Narrative: Theory and Practice,* Harvard English Studies 1 (Cambridge, Mass., 1970), p. 122.

6. Although Hatfield gives each section of the sequence a separate number, the thematic and tonal connections among the different parts, as well as the composition of the whole on the same manuscript, indicate that Brontë was working with an extended, episodic unit.

7. #57, then, is a shorter draft of "Douglas's Ride." Fannie Ratchford makes the same connection between the two poems, but she feels that their events follow the murder of Augusta—when Douglas is seriously hurt. See *Gondal's Queen,* p. 156.

8. Elizabeth Gaskell quotes Charlotte on Emily's love of liberty in *The Life of Charlotte Brontë,* p. 90.

9. *Wuthering Heights,* ch. 15, p. 134. And see J. Hillis Miller, "Emily Brontë," *The Disappearance of God* (Cambridge, Mass., 1963): "For Emily Brontë no human being is self-sufficient, and all suffering derives ultimately from isolation." Hence, the self seeks to escape "from the prison of its finitude" (p. 172).

10. The phrase comes from *The Mill on the Floss,* Book I, chapter 5.

11. Derek Stanford notes this polarity between the visions of day and night, and outlines its development in the Romantic metaphysical tradition preceding Brontë's poems. See *Emily Brontë: Her Life and Work,* pp. 192–97.

12. Herbert Dingle, *The Mind of Emily Brontë* (London, 1974), p. 42.

13. Inga-Stina Ewbank, p. 106.

14. Six months separate "Ah! why, because the dazzling sun" and "Julian M. and A. G. Rochelle," whose respective dates are April 14 and October 9, 1845. Only three poems—one of them unfinished and one undated—follow "Julian M. and A. G. Rochelle" in Hatfield's edition.

15. *Wuthering Heights,* ch. 34, p. 259.

16. This poem is not dated, and Hatfield does not give it an entry number. In his prefatory note to the poem, Hatfield suggests that it may have been written by Charlotte, who meant it to pass as Emily's when she added it to a selection of poems that were published with the 1850 edition of *Wuthering Heights.* Hatfield's judgment is not to be taken lightly, but in this instance it seems unfounded. The quality of the poem, its diction and theme, are Emily's at her best and show little evidence of Charlotte's presence.

Chapter Four

1. Lawrence and E. M. Hanson, *The Four Brontës* (London and New York, 1949), p. 121.

2. Gaskell, pp. 151–52.

3. Fannie E. Ratchford, "Introduction" to *Five Essays Written in French by Emily Jane Brontë,* trans. Lorine White Nagel (Folcroft, Pa., 1974), p. 7—originally published by the University of Texas Press in 1948. I use this source, referred to in my text as *Essays in French,* for the five essays it translates. All seven essays, in the original French, can be found in Gérin, pp. 266–74, from which I translate "Lettre" and "The Palace of Death" and will footnote.

4. This passage from chapter 3 of *The Origin of Species* is reprinted in *Darwin,* A Norton Critical Edition, ed. Philip Appleman (New York: W. W. Norton and Company, 1970), p. 116. The Tennyson reference is to *In Memoriam,* #56.

5. *King Lear,* Act IV, scene 1, ll. 38–39.

6. The "Epistle to John Hamilton Reynolds" appears in most modern editions of Keats's poetry. Written on March 25, 1818, the "Epistle" was not published until 1848, and thus would have been unknown to Brontë, but there were numerous foreshadowings of the Darwinian theory in the literature of the eighteenth and early nineteenth centuries. J. Hillis Miller notes the close resemblance to Brontë's view of the struggle for existence in one of John Wesley's sermons. See *The Disappearance of God* (Cambridge, Mass., 1963), p. 164, n. 11.

7. See Jo Anne A. Willson, " 'The Butterfly' and *Wuthering Heights*: A Mystic's Eschatology," *Victorian Newsletter* 33 (Spring 1968):24.

8. On the same day that Emily wrote "The Butterfly," August 11, 1842, Charlotte wrote an essay called "The Caterpillar." Though obviously drawn from the same source as Emily's, Charlotte's essay is very different. It deals explicitly and entirely with the parallels between the caterpillar and man's material life, and the butterfly and man's spiritual life. More conventionally religious than Emily's, it makes no mention at all of the struggle for existence. "The Caterpillar" has been translated by Phyllis Bentley in "New Brontë Devoirs," *Brontë Society Transactions* 12 (1955):362–64.

9. See Willson, pp. 22–25; and Miller, pp. 163–211, passim.

10. "Lettre" is in Gérin, pp. 268–69. It has been translated by Phyllis Bentley in "New Brontë Devoirs," p. 384.

11. "Le Palais de la Mort" in Gérin, pp. 272–74. It has been translated by Margaret Lane in "French Essays by Charlotte and Emily," *Brontë Society Transactions* 12 (1954):280–84.

12. *The Complete Poems of Emily Jane Brontë,* #178, p. 213.

13. In *The Disappearance of God,* J. Hillis Miller states that Emily Brontë, like the Calvinistic Methodist George Whitefield, "emphasizes man's penchant for sin, and the seemingly Godforsaken situation of many men" (p. 185). Neither in the essays nor in her other literature, however, does Brontë clearly reveal what her religious beliefs were, and we can only speculate on them. The view of man's fallen, morally helpless nature in "The Palace of Death" finds its opposite in Brontë's faith in the powerful God within her breast of "No coward soul is mine."

Chapter Five

1. The review, one of the five that were found in Brontë's desk, appeared in the *Examiner* and is included in *The Brontës: The Critical Heritage,* ed. Miriam Allott (London and Boston, 1974), pp. 220–22. *Wuthering Heights* disturbed most of its early reviewers, but as Miriam Allott points out (pp. 29–30), they were on the whole responsive to its power and potential.

2. May Sinclair, *The Three Brontës* (Boston and New York, 1912), p. 246.

3. Dorothy Van Ghent, "On *Wuthering Heights,*" *The English Novel: Form and Function* (New York, 1961; first published in 1953), p. 153.

4. As Terry Eagleton observes in *Myths of Power: A Marxist Study of the Brontës* (London, 1975), p. 100, "No mere critical hair-splitting can account for the protracted debate over whether Heathcliff is hero or demon, Catherine tragic heroine or spoiled brat, Nelly Dean shrewd or stupid. The narrative techniques of the novel are deliberately framed to preserve these ambivalences."

5. For the various literary sources that Brontë may have drawn upon in *Wuthering Heights,* see Florence Swinton Dry, *The Sources of Wuthering Heights* (Cambridge, England, 1937), pp. 1–48; and J. F. Goodridge, "A New Heaven and a New Earth," *The Art of Emily Brontë,* ed. Anne Smith (New York, 1976), pp. 160–81. Dry shows some convincing parallels between *Wuthering Heights* and Scott's *The Black Dwarf,* a story of thwarted love and revenge.

6. "The Bridegroom of Barna," *Blackwood's Magazine* 48 (November 1840):680–704.

7. Although I concentrate on the timeless or universal qualities of *Wuthering Heights,* other critics have remarked on its concerns with the social realities of England in the 1840s. In his chapter on *Wuthering Heights,* in *An Introduction to the English Novel* (London, 1951), 1:139–55, Arnold Kettle

argues that the Transcendentalist approach to Brontë's novel obscures its portrait of the conflicts and struggles that resulted from the Industrial Revolution and capitalism. Terry Eagleton advances a similar view in *Myths of Power,* pp. 97–121, but is more willing to admit the mythical and timeless aspects of *Wuthering Heights.*

8. Charles Percy Sanger, "The Structure of *Wuthering Heights,*" reprinted in the Norton Critical Edition of *Wuthering Heights,* ed. William M. Sale, Jr. (New York, 1963), pp. 286–98. Sanger's essay, first published in 1926, is one of the best known and most useful on *Wuthering Heights,* and, in addition to the genealogical chart, it lists the chronological dates of the story's events.

9. The page numbers are from the Norton Critical Edition. Because of the many available editions of *Wuthering Heights,* I also include chapter number for ease of reference.

10. David Cecil, in a very influential essay, quotes the argument between Cathy and Linton to define the opposition in the novel in terms of a "principle of storm" and a "principle of calm." See his chapter on Emily Brontë in *Victorian Novelists: Essays in Revaluation* (Chicago, 1958; first published in 1935 as *Early Victorian Novelists*), pp. 141–43. Dorothy Van Ghent speaks of the "tension between two kinds of reality" in *Wuthering Heights*: "the raw, inhuman reality of anonymous natural energies, and the restrictive reality of civilized habits, manners, and codes" (*The English Novel: Form and Function,* p. 157). In an original and insightful essay, Thomas A. Vogler discusses two modes of vision in *Wuthering Heights,* which result in two stories: one historical, chronological, threading through time; the other circular, discontinuous, mythic. His essay, "Story and History in *Wuthering Heights,*" is included in *Twentieth Century Interpretations of Wuthering Heights, A Collection of Critical Essays,* ed. Thomas A. Vogler (Englewood Cliffs, N.J., 1968), pp. 78–99.

11. A very good essay on the relativity of the characters' perceptions and the resulting clash among them is David Sonstroem, "*Wuthering Heights* and the Limits of Vision," *PMLA* 86 (January 1971):51–62.

12. I agree with Q. D. Leavis, in "A Fresh Approach to *Wuthering Heights,*" *Lectures in America* (New York, 1969), that Lockwood's "savage response to the ghost-child's plea for compassion is instinctive; so that under the civilized surface there is a Wuthering Heights self buried" (p. 125). Lockwood's role and the thematic importance of his dreams have received much critical attention, but I think it is wrong to reduce Lockwood, as a number of critics do, to an inept buffoon.

13. This is the view of Catherine's decision that most critics take. For them the choice between Heathcliff and Edgar becomes a very unequal one

between a complete man and a half-man, a true and a false version of reality. "She has gone far from reality when she is dazzled by the glittering glass-drops and the illusion of Thrushcross Grange," May Sinclair says of Catherine. "She has divorced her body from her soul for a little finer living, for a polished, a scrupulously clean, perfectly presentable husband" (*The Three Brontës,* p. 262). I think the choice is more difficult and equal than that, and Catherine's plight is defined more accurately by Q. D. Leavis as "a tragedy of being caught between socially incompatible cultures, for each of which there is much to be said, for and against" ("A Fresh Approach to *Wuthering Heights,"* p. 134). Leavis, on the other hand, gives Heathcliff scant importance in the story.

14. Other critics have noted the similarity between "No coward soul" and the language of Catherine's address to Nelly. I am most indebted to J. Hillis Miller, *The Disappearance of God.* For Miller, Catherine's "relation to Heathcliff gives her possession not merely of Heathcliff, but of the entire universe through him, in an intimacy of possession which obliterates the boundaries of the self and makes it an integral part of the whole creation" (p. 174). Keith Sagar is very good on what Catherine means when she says that Heathcliff is necessary to her. See "The Originality of *Wuthering Heights," in The Art of Emily Brontë,* ed. Anne Smith, pp. 146–47.

15. A number of theories have been offered to explain or account for the bond between Heathcliff and Catherine, although (or perhaps because), as Arnold Kettle observes, "It is not easy to suggest with any precision the quality of feeling that binds [them]" (*Introduction to the English Novel,* p. 142). Kettle's view is that their "affinity is forged" in their rebellion against Hindley's oppressive and degrading treatment of them (p. 143). Taking a Freudian approach, Thomas Moser, in "What Is the Matter with Emily Jane? Conflicting Impulses in *Wuthering Heights," Nineteenth-Century Fiction* 17 (June 1962):1–19, identifies Heathcliff as the id, a sexual force that awakens a sexual response in Catherine. Dorothy Van Ghent, however, probably speaks for the majority of critics when she says that Catherine and Heathcliff's love is not sexual, and that their passion for each other is characteristic of childhood rather than adulthood (*The English Novel: Form and Function,* pp. 158–59). Clifford Collins calls their love a "life-force relationship" rooted in nature and the unconscious, rather than society and the conscious self. His essay, "Theme and Conventions in *Wuthering Heights,"* is reprinted from the *Critic* in the 1963 Norton Critical Edition of *Wuthering Heights,* pp. 309–18; but it was not included in the Revised Norton Edition, published in 1972. In "The Incest Theme in *Wuthering Heights," Nineteenth-Century Fiction* 14 (June 1959): 80–83, Eric Solomon suggests an incestuous relation between the two, with Heathcliff being Mr. Earnshaw's illegitimate son and hence

Catherine's half-brother—but there is slim evidence to support this theory.

16. This is John K. Mathison's conclusion in "Nelly Dean and the Power of *Wuthering Heights*," *Nineteenth-Century Fiction* 11 (September 1956):107. For Mathison, however, Nelly is an admirable, wholesome woman.

17. James Hafley, "The Villain in *Wuthering Heights*," *Nineteenth-Century Fiction* 13 (December 1958):199–215.

18. See Emilio De Grazia, "The Ethical Dimension of *Wuthering Heights*," *Midwest Quarterly* 19 (Winter 1978):183. "While *Wuthering Heights* is a history of men alienated from each other, nature, and God, its thematic foundation is a faith that urges towards union are stronger than attempts to keep the human family separated."

19. Joseph Campbell describes the Yang/Yin symbol in *The Hero with a Thousand Faces* (New York: Meridian Books, 1956), p. 152.

20. Cecil, p. 155. Especially pertinent to my discussion of the second generation are Robert C. McKibben, "The Image of the Book in *Wuthering Heights*," *Nineteenth-Century Fiction* 15 (September 1960):159–69; and Miriam Allott, "The Rejection of Heathcliff?" *Wuthering Heights: A Casebook*, ed. Miriam Allott (London, 1970), pp. 183–206.

21. There are, on the other hand, critics who feel that the second half of *Wuthering Heights* is a weaker, toned-down version of the energies displayed in the first half. Richard Chase advanced this view—that in both *Jane Eyre* and *Wuthering Heights*, a moderate Victorian domesticity triumphs over a primitive, masculine sexual force—in "The Brontës, or, Myth Domesticated," *Forms of Modern Fiction*, ed. William Van O'Conner (Minneapolis, 1948), pp. 102–19. Chase's argument is seconded by Thomas Moser, who claims that Hareton is emasculated by Cathy, and that eventually "all Wuthering Heights suffers feminization" ("What Is the Matter with Emily Jane?", p. 15).

22. Q. D. Leavis, p. 96.

23. I am quoting from "Julian M. and A. G. Rochelle," #190, p. 239, in Hatfield's edition of Brontë's *Complete Poems*.

Chapter Six

1. See Melvin R. Watson's survey of the criticism of *Wuthering Heights* in "*Wuthering Heights* and the Critics," *Trollopian* (later renamed *Nineteenth-Century Fiction*) 3 (March 1949):243–63. Although Watson regards Sanger's essay as a turning point in Emily Brontë criticism, he also notes that it did not put an end to inadequate, unhelpful studies of Brontë or her work.

2. Lascelles Abercrombie, "The Brontës Today," *Brontë Society Transactions* 6 (1924):195–96. Abercrombie compares Emily Brontë to Conrad.

3. F. B. Pinion, *A Brontë Companion: Literary Assessment, Background, and Reference* (London, 1975), p. 204.

4. Swinburne's essay, a review of Mary Robinson's *Emily Brontë*, appeared in the *Athenaeum,* June 1883, and is reprinted in *The Brontës: The Critical Heritage,* ed. Miriam Allott (London and Boston, 1974), pp. 438–44; see p. 444. David P. Drew, in "Emily Brontë and Emily Dickinson as Mystic Poets," *Brontë Society Transactions* 15 (1968), states "there is little doubt that Dickinson read and was influenced by *Wuthering Heights* and the earlier published Brontë verse" (p. 227).

Selected Bibliography

PRIMARY SOURCES

The Complete Poems of Emily Jane Brontë. Edited by C. W. Hatfield. New York: Columbia University Press, 1941.

Five Essays Written in French by Emily Jane Brontë. Trans. Lorine White Nagel. Austin, 1948; rpt. Folcroft, Pa.: Folcroft Library Editions, 1974.

Wuthering Heights. Edited By Hilda Marsden and Ian Jack. Oxford: The Clarendon Press, 1978. An excellent scholarly edition, with informative notes, textual variants, and supplemental essays.

Wuthering Heights: An Authoritative Text with Essays in Criticism. Edited by William M. Sale, Jr. New York: W. W. Norton and Company, 1963; 2nd ed. 1972. One of the best of the easily accessible editions of *Wuthering Heights.*

Bentley, Phyllis. "New Brontë Devoirs." *Brontë Society Transactions* 12 (1955):361–85. Includes a translation of Brontë's essay "Lettre."

Lane, Margaret. "French Essays by Charlotte and Emily." *Brontë Society Transactions* 12 (1954):273–85. Includes a translation of Brontë's essay "The Palace of Death."

Shorter, Clement. *The Brontës: Life and Letters.* 2 vols. London: Hodder and Stoughton, 1908. Principally letters by and about the Brontës—especially Charlotte.

Wise, Thomas J., and Symington, J. A., eds. *The Brontës: Their Lives, Friendships and Correspondence.* 4 vols. Oxford: The Shakespeare Head Press, 1932. More complete than Shorter, and the standard text for the Brontë correspondence, although scholars have noted its shortcomings.

SECONDARY SOURCES

1. Bibliography

Barclay, Janet M. *Emily Brontë Criticism, 1900–1968: An Annotated Check List.* New York: Astor, Lenox and Tilden Foundations and Readex

Books, 1974. An excellent bibliography of Emily Brontë criticism from 1900 to 1968, with very helpful annotations.

Christian, Mildred G. "The Brontës." In *Victorian Fiction: A Guide to Research*. Edited by Lionel Stevenson. Cambridge: Harvard University Press, 1964, pp. 214–44. A selective, reliable review essay on the primary and secondary material pertaining to the Brontës through 1962.

Passel, Anne. *Charlotte and Emily Brontë: An Annotated Bibliography*. New York and London: Garland Publishing, Inc., 1979. The most recent and thorough bibliography of works by and about the Brontës, systematically arranged—indispensable for future Brontë studies.

Rosengarten, Herbert J. "The Brontës." In *Victorian Fiction: A Second Guide to Research*. Edited by George H. Ford. New York: The Modern Language Association of America, 1978, pp. 172–203. A sequel to Christian's essay in the Stevenson volume; covers the years 1963–1974.

2. Biography

Chadwick, Mrs. Ellis H. *In the Footsteps of the Brontës*. London: Sir Isaac Pitman and Sons, 1914. Contains a great deal of information about the Brontës and their family history; Emily's stay at Law Hill is considered in detail.

Gaskell, Elizabeth. *The Life of Charlotte Brontë*. 1857; rpt. Everyman's Library. London: J. M. Dent and Co., n.d. The classic biography of Charlotte and an invaluable source of material about Emily.

Gérin, Winifred. *Emily Brontë: A Biography*. Oxford: Clarendon Press, 1971. The most informative modern biography.

Hanson, Lawrence, and Hanson, E. M. *The Four Brontës: The Lives and Works of Charlotte, Branwell, Emily, and Anne Brontë*. London: Oxford University Press, 1949. A good, general study of the Brontës, with an extensive bibliography.

Nussey, Ellen. "Reminiscences of Charlotte Brontë." *Scribner's Monthly* 2 (May 1871):18–31. Includes a rare firsthand description of Emily.

Robinson, A. Mary F. *Emily Brontë*. London: W. H. Allen and Co., 1883. The earliest biography, with information derived from people who remembered Brontë.

Simpson, Charles. *Emily Brontë*. London, 1929; rpt. Folcroft, Pa.: Folcroft Library Editions, 1977. A sensible and well-balanced biography.

3. Criticism

Abercrombie, Lascelles. "The Brontës Today." *Brontë Society Transactions* 6

(1924):179–200. One of the first serious criticisms of *Wuthering Heights* as a work of art.

Allott, Miriam, ed. *The Brontës: The Critical Heritage.* London and Boston: Routledge and Kegan Paul, 1974. Excellent collection of Brontë criticism and reviews from 1846 to 1900; a helpful reference for Emily's reception by Victorian critics.

Allott, Miriam. "The Rejection of Heathcliff?" In *Wuthering Heights: A Casebook.* Edited by Miriam Allott. London: Macmillan and Company, 1970, pp. 183–206. Brontë has to reject Heathcliff and create "a new order out of a judicious combination of Lintons and Earnshaws."

Apter, T. E. "Romanticism and Romantic Love in *Wuthering Heights.*" In *The Art of Emily Brontë.* Edited by Anne Smith. New York: Barnes and Noble, 1976, pp. 205–222. Hareton and Cathy provide an effective alternative to the Romantic intensity and destructiveness of Heathcliff and Catherine.

Blondel, Jacques. *Emily Brontë: Experience Spirituelle et Création Poétique.* Paris: Presses Universitaires de France, 1955. A comprehensive study of Brontë's background, the poems, and *Wuthering Heights.* Written in French.

Bradner, Leicester. "The Growth of *Wuthering Heights.*" *PMLA* 48 (March 1933):129–46. Discusses the possible sources for *Wuthering Heights* in the literature Brontë read and in her poems.

Burns, Wayne. "In Death They Were Not Divided: The Moral Magnificence of Unmoral Passion in *Wuthering Heights.*" *Hartford Studies in Literature* 5 (1973):135–59. Argues that the love between Heathcliff and Catherine is "immaculate" rather than sexual, and can be consummated only in death.

Cecil, David. *Victorian Novelists: Essays in Revaluation.* 1935; rpt. Chicago: University of Chicago Press, 1958. Contains one of the major essays on *Wuthering Heights* as a metaphysical or cosmic novel divided between the principle of storm and the principle of calm.

Chase, Richard. "The Brontës, or, Myth Domesticated." In *Forms of Modern Fiction: Essays Collected in Honor of Joseph Warren Beach.* Edited by William Van O'Conner. Minneapolis: The University of Minnesota Press, 1948, pp. 102–19. Discusses the Brontës' use of myth; in *Jane Eyre* and *Wuthering Heights,* a moderate Victorian domesticity triumphs over a primitive, masculine sexual force.

Craik, W. A. *The Brontë Novels.* London: Metheun and Co., 1968. The chapter on *Wuthering Heights* has good insights into the relationship between Catherine and Heathcliff.

Cunningham, Valentine. *Everywhere Spoken Against: Dissent in the Victorian Novel.* Oxford: The Clarendon Press, 1975. Discusses the influence of Methodism on the lives and works of the Brontës (pp. 113–26).

Daiches, David. "Introduction." *Wuthering Heights.* London: Penquin Books, 1965, pp. 7–29. A good general interpretation of *Wuthering Heights,* pointing out the strong effect Brontë gains by treating her extraordinary characters so matter-of-factly.

De Grazia, Emilio. "The Ethical Dimension of *Wuthering Heights.*" *Midwest Quarterly* 19 (Winter 1978):176–95. Very good essay on the moral system—the meaning of good and evil—which Brontë explores in her novel.

Dingle, Herbert. *The Mind of Emily Brontë.* London: Martin Brian and O'Keeffe, 1974. An attempt to "delineate the type of mind" that could produce Brontë's writings, and to distinguish Brontë the writer from Brontë the person.

Dodds, Madeleine Hope. "Gondaliand." *Modern Language Review* 18 (January 1923):9–21. One of the pioneer articles on the Gondal literature; though now outdated, it has worthwhile insights into Brontë's methods.

————. "Heathcliff's Country." *Modern Language Review* 39 (April 1944):116–29. A reconstruction of the Gondal story.

Donoghue, Denis. "Emily Brontë: On the Latitude of Interpretation." In *The Interpretation of Narrative: Theory and Practice.* Harvard English Studies 1. Edited by Morton W. Bloomfield. Cambridge, Mass.: Harvard University Press, 1970, pp. 105–33. One of the best essays on Brontë's thought and her Romanticism, especially in her poetry.

Drew, David P. "Emily Brontë and Emily Dickinson as Mystical Poets." *Brontë Society Transactions* 15 (1968):227–32. Notes the similarities in the mystical quality of the two poets.

Drew, Philip. "Charlotte Brontë as a Critic of *Wuthering Heights.*" *Nineteenth-Century Fiction* 18 (March 1964):365–81. A persuasive essay, arguing that Heathcliff has sold his soul to the devil for the power to gain Catherine back.

Dry, Florence Swinton. *The Sources of Wuthering Heights.* Cambridge, England: W. Heffer and Sons, 1937. An important source study of *Wuthering Heights*; a number of parallels suggest that Brontë drew upon Walter Scott's *The Black Dwarf.*

Eagleton, Terry. *Myths of Power: A Marxist Study of the Brontës.* London: The Macmillan Press, 1975. An illuminating chapter on *Wuthering Heights* interprets it in terms of a class struggle between the landed gentry and the new capitalism.

Ewbank, Inga-Stina. *Their Proper Sphere: A Study of the Brontë Sisters as Early-Victorian Female Novelists.* London: Edward Arnold Ltd., 1966. One of the best books on the Brontës; Emily is preeminently a poetic writer, able to accommodate opposing attitudes and judgments within individual poems and her novel.

Goodridge, J. F. "A New Heaven and a New Earth." In *The Art of Emily Brontë*. Edited by Anne Smith. New York: Barnes and Noble, 1976, pp. 160–81. Discusses possible literary traditions and sources behind *Wuthering Heights*.

Grove, Robin. "'It Would Not Do': Emily Brontë as Poet." In *The Art of Emily Brontë*. Edited by Anne Smith. New York: Barnes and Noble, 1976, pp. 33–67. Argues that much of Brontë's poetry was derivative and that it became a means of "sealing-off the self from the demands of the adult world."

Hafley, James. "The Villain in *Wuthering Heights*." *Nineteenth-Century Fiction* 13 (December 1958):199–215. Argues that the villain is Nelly Dean.

Hardy, Barbara. "The Lyricism of Emily Brontë." In *The Art of Emily Brontë*. Edited by Anne Smith. New York: Barnes and Noble, 1976, pp. 94–118. A carefully reasoned study of the poems about imagination.

Hewish, John. *Emily Brontë: A Critical and Biographical Study*. London: Macmillan and Co., 1969. A very good book, with a judicious biographical outline and a discussion of *Wuthering Heights* from several perspectives; includes a detailed account of early *Wuthering Heights* criticism and an extensive bibliography.

Hinkley, Laura L. *The Brontës: Charlotte and Emily*. London: Hammond, Hammond and Co., 1947. Goes over the basic Brontë story, but with original interpretations of Emily's character and work, and a reconstruction of the Gondal story.

Kettle, Arnold. *An Introduction to the English Novel*. Vol. 1. London: Hutchinson University Library, 1951. A Marxist interpretation of *Wuthering Heights*, stressing its concern with concrete social realities, as opposed to Transcendental or Romantic themes (pp. 139–55).

Kiely, Robert. *The Romantic Novel in England*. Cambridge, Mass.: Harvard University Press, 1972. "*Wuthering Heights* is the masterpiece of English romantic fiction," and is studied in the context of the Gothic tradition (pp. 235–51).

Knoepflmacher, U. C. *Laughter and Despair: Readings in Ten Novels of the Victorian Era*. Berkeley and Los Angeles: University of California Press, 1971. In *Wuthering Heights*, Brontë fuses pessimism and hope, tragedy and comedy, and is able to resist the formulas by which her characters want to reduce reality (pp. 84–108).

Krupat, Arnold. "The Strangeness of *Wuthering Heights*." *Nineteenth-Century Fiction* 25 (December 1970):269–80. The strangeness lies in the disparity between the events described and the plain, familiar language Lockwood and Nelly use to describe them.

Leavis, Q. D. "A Fresh Approach to *Wuthering Heights*." In *Lectures in America*. By F. R. and Q. D. Leavis. New York: Pantheon Books, 1969, pp. 83–152. A substantial criticism; minimizes the importance of Heathcliff and stresses the realism and central human concerns of the story.

Lewis, C. Day. "Emily Brontë and Freedom." In *Notable Images of Virtue*. Toronto: The Ryerson Press, 1954, pp. 1–25. Traces the images of freedom in the poems.

Mathison, John K. "Nelly Dean and the Power of *Wuthering Heights*." *Nineteenth-Century Fiction* 11 (September 1956):106–29. Nelly's common sense keeps her from understanding characters like Heathcliff and Catherine.

McKibben, Robert C. "The Image of the Book in *Wuthering Heights*." *Nineteenth-Century Fiction* 15 (September 1960):159–69. Contrasts the misuse of books in the first generation with the unifying power of books in the second generation.

Miles, Rosalind. "A Baby God: The Creative Dynamism of Emily Brontë's Poetry." In *The Art of Emily Brontë*. Edited by Anne Smith. New York: Barnes and Noble, 1976, pp. 68–93. A good analysis of the style and language of the poems.

Miller, J. Hillis. *The Disappearance of God*. Cambridge, Mass.: Harvard University Press, 1963. A major study of the religious meanings and implications of Brontë's work (pp. 157–211).

Morgan, Charles. *Reflections In a Mirror*. London: Macmillan and Co., 1944. Includes a chapter on Brontë that analyzes the mystical quality of the poems and *Wuthering Heights*.

Morgan, Edwin. "Women and Poetry." *Cambridge Journal* 3 (August 1950):643–73. The essence of Brontë's art is directness and particularity, with a refusal to generalize and draw conclusions.

Moser, Thomas. "What Is the Matter with Emily Jane? Conflicting Impulses in *Wuthering Heights*." *Nineteenth-Century Fiction* 17 (June 1962):1–19. A Freudian approach; argues that the sexual force symbolized in Heathcliff is tamed in the next generation.

Ohmann, Carol. "Emily Brontë in the Hands of Male Critics." *College English* 32 (May 1971):906–13. Attitudes toward *Wuthering Heights* changed when it was discovered its author was a woman, and sexual prejudice continues to influence readers' responses to Brontë and her novel.

Paden, W. D. *An Investigation of Gondal*. New York: Bookman Associates, 1958. A scholarly reconstruction of the Gondal story, carefully distinguishing between the provable and the probable.

Patterson, Charles I., Jr. "Empathy and the Daemonic in *Wuthering Heights*." In *The English Novel in the Nineteenth-Century: Essays on the Mediation of Human Values*. Edited by George Goodin. Urbana: University of Illinois Press, 1972, pp. 81–96. A metaphysical interpretation, arguing that Brontë fuses the daemonic and the human in Catherine and Heathcliff.

Pinion, F. B. *A Brontë Companion: Literary Assessment, Background, and Reference.* London: The Macmillan Press, 1975. A useful guide to the Brontës for the general reader, with separate chapters on Emily's poems and *Wuthering Heights.*

Ratchford, Fannie Elizabeth. *The Brontës' Web of Childhood.* New York: Columbia University Press, 1941. The basic study of the Brontës' early writings; traces the growth of the Angrian and Gondal stories.

————. *Gondal's Queen: A Novel in Verse by Emily Jane Brontë.* Austin: University of Texas Press, 1955. Arranges the Gondal poems to form a story centering on Augusta Almeda; valuable Introduction and Appendixes.

Sagar, Keith. "The Originality of *Wuthering Heights.*" In *The Art of Emily Brontë.* Edited by Anne Smith. New York: Barnes and Noble, 1976, pp. 121–59. Brontë's art encompassed the whole of her experience, including areas, such as the unconscious, closed to her contemporaries.

Sanger, Charles Percy. "The Structure of *Wuthering Heights.*" 1926; rpt. The Norton Critical Edition of *Wuthering Heights.* Edited by William M. Sale, Jr. New York: W. W. Norton and Company, 1963; 2nd ed. 1972, pp. 286–98. A major essay; provides a detailed chronology of the novel's events, and demonstrates the precision with which Brontë worked out the law of inheritance.

Shapiro, Arnold. "*Wuthering Heights* as a Victorian Novel." *Studies in the Novel* 1 (Fall 1969):284–96. *Wuthering Heights* belongs to "the same ethical and moral tradition as the other great Victorian novels"; it supports a teacher-pupil relationship over that of master and slave.

Sinclair, May. *The Three Brontës.* Boston and New York: Houghton Mifflin Company, 1912. One of the best of the early studies of the Brontës; treats Emily and her work in detail.

Solomon, Eric. "The Incest Theme in *Wuthering Heights.*" *Nineteenth-Century Fiction* 14 (June 1959):80–83. Suggests that Heathcliff is Mr. Earnshaw's illegitimate son and Catherine's half-brother.

Sonstroem, David. "*Wuthering Heights* and the Limits of Vision." *PMLA* 86 (January 1971):51–62. A very good essay; argues that the conflict stems from the relativity and inadequacy of the characters' perceptions.

Spark, Muriel, and Stanford, Derek. *Emily Brontë: Her Life and Work.* New York: Coward-McCann, 1966. Biographical section by Spark; critical section by Stanford covers the poems well.

Starzyk, Lawrence J. "Emily Brontë: Poetry in a Mingled Tone." *Criticism* 14 (Spring 1972):119–36. Stresses the bleak view in the poetry of external nature and man's inner psyche.

Tristam, Philippa. "Divided Sources." In *The Art of Emily Brontë*. Edited by Anne Smith. New York: Barnes and Noble, 1976, pp. 182–204. Discusses the patterns of innocence and experience—childhood and maturity—as they appear in the two generations of *Wuthering Heights*.

Van de Laar, Elizabeth. *The Inner Structure of Wuthering Heights: A Study of an Imaginative Field*. The Hague: Mouton and Co., 1969. A systematic study of the images and image patterns in *Wuthering Heights*; notes the frequency with which each image is associated with each character.

Van Ghent, Dorothy. "On *Wuthering Heights*." In *The English Novel: Form and Function*. 1953; rpt. New York: Harper Torchbooks Edition, 1961, pp. 153–70. Very good essay; shows the persistence of the window image and its importance to the concepts of self and otherness.

Vargish, Thomas. "Revenge and *Wuthering Heights*." *Studies in the Novel* 3 (Spring 1971):7–17. Heathcliff uses revenge to make the second generation recreate and parody the events of his past.

Visick, Mary. *The Genesis of Wuthering Heights*. Hong Kong: Hong Kong University Press, 1958. Traces the evolution of *Wuthering Heights* from the characters and conflicts of the Gondal poems.

Vogler, Thomas A. "Story and History in *Wuthering Heights*." In *Twentieth Century Interpretations of Wuthering Heights: A Collection of Critical Essays*. Edited by Thomas A. Vogler. Englewood Cliffs, N.J.: Prentice-Hall, Inc., 1968, pp. 78–99. An insightful essay, distinguishing two "stories"—two modes of vision—in *Wuthering Heights*.

Watson, Melvin R. "*Wuthering Heights* and the Critics." *Trollopian* 3 (March 1949):243–63. Very good critical survey of the literature on *Wuthering Heights* for the first one hundred years after its appearance.

Willis, Irene Cooper. *The Authorship of Wuthering Heights*. London: The Hogarth Press, 1936. Studies the style of *Wuthering Heights* closely, and contrasts it with that of Charlotte and Branwell to refute the notion that either of them could have written *Wuthering Heights*.

Willson, Jo Anne A. " 'The Butterfly' and *Wuthering Heights*: A Mystic's Eschatology." *Victorian Newsletter* 33 (Spring 1968):22–25. The theme of death and new life, which Brontë develops in her novel, can be found in her Brussels essay on the butterfly.

Winnifrith, Tom. *The Brontës and Their Background: Romance and Reality*. London: The Macmillan Press, 1973. Separate chapters discuss such topics as textual problems, religious influences, and "The Brontës and their Books"; a fresh approach to ideas that influenced the Brontës and to the history of their reputation.

Woodring, Carl R. "The Narrators of *Wuthering Heights*." *Nineteenth-Century Fiction* 11 (March 1957):298–305. Lockwood, the stranger to the Heights, and Nelly, the intimate, provide different perspectives onto the story—one detached, the other involved.

Index